# A Primer on
# Corporate Governance

# A Primer on Corporate Governance

## Turkey

Sibel Yamak and Bengi Ertuna

BEP BUSINESS EXPERT PRESS

*A Primer on Corporate Governance: Turkey*

First published in 2017 by
Business Expert Press, LLC
222 East 46th Street, New York, NY 10017
www.businessexpertpress.com

ISBN-13: 978-1-60649-882-8 (paperback)
ISBN-13: 978-1-60649-883-5 (e-book)

Business Expert Press Corporate Governance Collection

Collection ISSN: 1948-0470 (print)
Collection ISSN: 1948-0415 (electronic)

Cover and interior design by Exeter Premedia Services Private Ltd., Chennai, India

First edition: 2017

10 9 8 7 6 5 4 3 2 1

Printed in the United States of America.

# Abstract

*A Primer on Corporate Governance: Turkey* takes an in-depth and comprehensive assessment of corporate governance in Turkey, at a cross section in time when the country is going through major multidimensional transformations.

Turkey is denoted as a country of contrasts with respect to its performance on economic and social dimensions. The recent changes in the economy as well as its structural characteristics are presented in the first part of the book. This is crucial for a holistic understanding of the Turkish business system embedded in a dynamic but at times erratic economic context that influences all the governance practices at public and private sectors. History is another dimension to fully grasp the essential traits of the business system and its governance attributes. Hence, the historical antecedents of Turkish corporate governance are provided to the readers as a background in the first part of the book. Building on this background, external and internal mechanisms of corporate governance are discussed in the subsequent chapters. Legal system of the country, its company laws, regulatory authorities, and the state of the market for corporate control, as well as the socio-cultural norms, ways of doing business, and the Turkish code of good governance are examined as the external mechanisms shaping the corporate governance practices of companies. Characteristics of the board of directors, ownership structure, and management teams of Turkish companies are analyzed as internal control mechanisms. The last part of the book includes a conclusion section, discussing current and future corporate governance challenges in the Turkish business context.

# Keywords

boards of directors, CEOs, emerging economy, history of Turkish corporate governance, ownership structure, state and governance, Turkey, Turkish business culture

# Contents

# Foreword

We had the initial thoughts about writing a book on "Corporate Governance in Turkey" with a holistic perspective when we were drafting a chapter on governance for an edited book by Alessandro Zattoni and William Judge. However, this thought has not materialized until we were invited by William Judge to contribute a book to Corporate Governance Series of BEP. We advocate for the contextual nature of corporate governance and the potential contribution of adopting a multilevel approach in taking up the unique challenges of the context.

Our multilevel assessment of corporate governance, taking into consideration the interactions of governance at global, institutional, organizational, and individual levels, can contribute to the endeavor of designing corporate governance solutions in other contexts as well, at a time when corporate governance is considered as a panacea for the challenging problems of globalization.

Adopting a multilevel approach also facilitates an analysis on the dynamics of corporate governance in a context. Thus, the diffusionist pressures at the global level, state-induced uncertainties at the institutional level, varying perceptions of corporate governance at the organizational level, and divergent views of managers and board members at the individual level provided us with a comprehensive view of contrasting forces in Turkish corporate governance and an assessment of its future challenges. Consequently, this book with its detailed analysis of a large number of dimensions like the history, business culture, legal infrastructure, media, company, and top executive characteristics among others aims to provide a rigorous overview of corporate governance in Turkey.

Although we were greatly satisfied about our broad coverage of the topic, the writing of a book on governance has been a real challenge in the continuously changing socio-political environment of Turkey. Growing government restrictions on media and its increasing interventions on economic institutions and companies and changing laws and regulations that threaten the property rights obliged us to revise our initial manuscript several times even within very short time frames to be able to reflect the actual situation. This itself supports the necessity of adopting a holistic view in governance analysis and thus investigating the contextual variables in force at different levels to understand a particular governance framework. It also indicates the unlikelihood of applying "one best governance structure" to every context.

This book is based on an extensive body of knowledge from the professional and scholarly research on corporate landscape in Turkey and our own cumulative research on Turkish companies. The aim is to provide a thorough understanding to those interested in or dealing with corporate governance practices in Turkey. Thus, it is intended for a broad audience including students and professors in graduate business schools together with practicing business executives and institutional investors.

# Acknowledgments

We would like to thank our colleagues and students who have taken a critical stance throughout our academic studies by questioning the misconceptions and dominant views in corporate governance research. We are indebted to our colleagues Aylin Ataay, Haluk Levent, and Ali Tükel for their careful reading and valuable contributions to the earlier versions of the book. We also extend our thanks to Elif Cemek for her assistance.

We would like to thank William Judge for having encouraged us to write this book which has been a truly enriching experience. We are grateful to Rob Zwettler for his understanding during the whole process. We are thankful to the Galatasaray University Research Fund for the support provided for this work.

We are grateful for the continuing support of Gulden Besler Sargin. Finally, we would like to express our gratitude to our families and especially to our children Ali Can, Elif, and Sinan, who have supported us throughout our scholarly work.

# PART I

# Overview of
# the Turkish Economy

# CHAPTER 1

# Economic Landscape of Companies

Turkey has a unique geographical location, being on the crossroads of Europe, North Africa, Middle East, and Central Asia, with ports on both the Mediterranean and Black Sea, acting as a bridge between Europe and Middle East, both geographically and culturally. While its strategic location between Europe, Middle East, and Russia offers opportunities for the country, it also poses challenges and risks as it is a part of one of the most unstable areas of the world. The population of the country was 78.7 million[1] as of the end of 2015, with favorable demographics, offering both the advantages of a young population together with pressing issues with respective job creation and public spending associated with building human capital and dealing with the challenges to be posed by aging population over the medium term.

Turkey is the 18th largest economy of the world in 2015 in gross domestic product (GDP) world rankings, with a GDP of 722 billion USD at current prices.[2] As displayed in Table 1.1, Turkey has displayed high rates of economic growth in the years after 2002. Although Turkey has achieved high rates of growth and has been denoted as an example in the international community to be emulated by other emerging markets, this achievement has been accompanied by uneven progress along various dimensions of economic and social development according to a World Bank report.[3] Many outsider observers designate Turkey as a "country of contrasts"[4] as they also take into consideration its uneven progress and contradictions in several areas. For example, Turkey liberalized its trade and capital flows, but its capital markets remained underdeveloped, as displayed in Table 1.3. In spite of the major urbanization process (share of the urban population reaching 73 percent in 2015),[5] traditional family structure and gender roles continued to persist. The country achieved a comprehensive harmonization of its laws and regulations with respect to the European Union (EU) standards; however, there are still significant concerns over the rule of law in the economy, discretionary and uneven application of regulations, and the governance in the public sector.[6] Turkey managed to achieve high growth rates, yet it was not able to generate sufficient productive employment.[7] While economic policy is pro-business and pro-investment, it is also protectionist at times and unpredictable.[8] It achieved remarkable success in poverty reduction and social inclusion over the last decade, considerably decreasing the inequality in access to basic social services, yet there are still concerns over access of the most vulnerable social groups to social services and sustainability of the social security system.[9]

In a study classifying emerging economies based on data from the Global Competitiveness Report of the World Economic Forum (WEF), Turkey is classified as a "mid-range emerging economy"[10] with a strong development of infrastructure and factor markets, and low institutional development. Going through "multiple transitions," Turkey has accomplished its transition from the "lower middle income" to the "higher middle income" category, and came close to the threshold of high income status economies; nonetheless, its performance has stagnated after 2011.[11] GDP growth, which was running above the average growth of the emerging market, has slowed down as a result of both the decrease in international demand following the 2009 global recession and the structural problems of the country with respect to international competitiveness.[12]

According to the Sustainable Governance Indicators[13] of Bertelsmann Stiftung, an institution publishing a cross-national comparative survey on the performance and governance capabilities of 41 countries including the Organization for European Economic Cooperation (OECD) and EU countries, Turkey falls into the "lower-middle class" category in 2015, ranking 23rd with respect to its performance on the economy dimension, when various dimensions including economic policy, labor markets, taxes, budgets, research and innovation, and global financial system are all taken into account. Even though Turkey has remarkable achievements in economic development, it has yet to establish the institutional requirements for becoming a high-income country.[14]

The transformations Turkey accomplished in the last three decades have been mainly led by the private sector and supported by a relatively recent political consensus on market-based outcomes.[15] However, Turkey's institutional context has been under the influence of its heritage, guiding the economy through state-desired allocations rather than market-based outcomes.[16] Moreover, this is a heritage not in compliance with the political consensus on market-based solutions. Turkey has consequently gone through a series of institutional reforms in the 1990s to develop a reliable economic framework for "arms' length transactions between the state and the private sector."[17] In spite of the fact that Turkey has achieved significant structural transformations often induced by external actors, institutional structure has yet to evolve in a reliable economic framework to foster competitiveness and sustainability in the business sector.

## Economic Development Paths

The economic progress of Turkey since the establishment of the Republic has incorporated major policy shifts, which have significantly influenced the structure of the Turkish business context and the performance of the companies. In all these periods, the role of the state was pivotal in shaping the business system. It is possible to identify periods of different regimes as determined by these policy shifts. Öniş and Senses[18] divide the post–World War II Turkish economic development into four phases with respect to the policy regime adopted. These developmental stages have had considerable impacts on the configuration of the business context.

The first phase refers to the period between 1950 and 1960 in which the Turkish economic policy moved from a state-led industrialization strategy to liberalization and integration with the world economy based on agriculture-led exports. In this period, expansion of agricultural land, mechanization, and agricultural support policies are observed in the agricultural sector, while industrialization is mainly based on consumer goods, such as food and textiles.

In the second phase, that is the period between 1960 and 1980, Turkey adopted an import substitution policy. Here the state was also a key driver of economic and social transformation. Restrictions to capital flows and controls over international trade characterized the period and provided opportunities for entrepreneurs having contract capabilities with international firms.[19] These entrepreneurs started manufacturing businesses and served the consumer demand in the protected domestic market by utilizing their international contracts and privileges provided by the state.[20] New industrial entrepreneurs, organized labor, and the empowered bureaucratic elite seem to characterize this period in which one can observe relatively high rates of growth and a significant structural transformation.

Turkey moved from an import substitution policy to an export-oriented policy and adopted liberalization policies in the third phase, namely in the period between 1980 and 2001. During this interval, the Turkish economy was shaped by a market-based model of development. Free market discourse and market mechanisms introduced with the macroeconomic stabilization and financial liberalization program of January 1980 took the center stage in 1990s.[21] In 1989, Turkey liberalized its capital account and integrated with the global financial markets. It also signed a customs union agreement with the European Union in 1996, ending the restrictions on capital flows and controls over international trade. Here Turkey increasingly became dependent on financial inflows, with the economy following cycles of boom and bust, represented by the crisis in 1994, and the twin crises of 2000 and 2001. With regard to this period in question, it is possible to pin down a loosening of organized labor and decrease in the regulatory capacities of the state.

The fourth phase of Turkish economic development relates to the period after 2001. Following the twin crises in 2000 and 2001, Turkey adopted an International Monetary Fund (IMF)-backed stabilization program. During this period, regulatory institutions in banking and finance improved, the Central Bank became independent, new bureaucratic institutions were established, and regulations were put into effect to support businesses and to make the business context more conducive for foreign investors. The stabilization program included a comprehensive privatization program also carried out in this period. Reforms undertaken after the financial crisis have certainly contributed to a period of economic growth and stability.[22]

Pamuk[23] claims that the major policy shifts Turkey has experienced during the last 200 years correspond to the dominant paradigm in the global economy in that period. This claim corroborates Öniş and Şenses's principal thesis[24] that Turkey pursues reactive state strategies, adopting the dominant norms and policies advocated by the major international decision-making centers of the world economic order.

## GDP Size and Income per Capita

GDP size in Turkey has increased almost 3.5 times from 231 billion in 2002 to 800 billion USD in 2014. This significant increase observed in the GDP size looks less inspiring when compared with the performance of the group of emerging market countries, of which Turkey is also a member. During the same period, the total GDP of the emerging countries has approximately increased 4.4 times from 6.9 trillion USD to 30.5 trillion USD.[25] It is also worth noting that increases in the GDP size have decreased after 2008, and the size of economy has in fact decreased from 823 billion dollars in 2013 to 800 billion dollars in 2014.

Per capita income displays a similar but a less favorable course. This figure has increased significantly from 3,492 USD in 2002 to 10,444 USD

*Table 1.1  The GDP size, the per capita income, and the GDP growth rate in the period between 2002 and 2014*

| Year | GDP (billion USD) | Per capita income (USD) | GDP growth rate (%) |
|---|---|---|---|
| 2002 | 231 | 3,492 | 6.2 |
| 2003 | 305 | 4,565 | 5.3 |
| 2004 | 390 | 5,775 | 9.4 |
| 2005 | 482 | 7,036 | 8.4 |
| 2006 | 526 | 7,597 | 6.9 |
| 2007 | 649 | 9,247 | 4.7 |
| 2008 | 742 | 10,444 | 0.7 |
| 2009 | 617 | 8,561 | −4.8 |
| 2010 | 732 | 10,003 | 9.2 |
| 2011 | 774 | 10,428 | 8.8 |
| 2012 | 786 | 10,459 | 2.2 |
| 2013 | 823 | 10,822 | 4.2 |
| 2014 | 800 | 10,404 | 2.9 |

*Source:* TÜİK [Turkish Statistical Institute][26] and the Undersecretariat of Treasury.[27]

in 2008. It has, however, stagnated around this level from then on. Developments in GDP, per capita income and GDP growth rates for the period between 2002 and 2014 are presented in Table 1.1.

# GDP Growth Trends

GDP growth rates have historically been volatile but generally moved in parallel to the global average. In his book focusing on the economic history of Turkey over the last 200 years, Pamuk[28] states that the per capita income has exhibited an increase corresponding to the world average, taking into account the whole period of the last 200 years. From the beginning of the 19th century up to the midst of the 20th century, per capita incomes have certainly increased but the discrepancy between the growth rates in Turkey and in developed countries has widened due to the rapid industrialization in developed countries. During the postwar period, this discrepancy did not disappear, though Turkey's growth rates have increased. In comparison to other emerging countries, Turkish economy has displayed faster growth rates in per capita income up to 1950s and slipped back to the average growth rate thereafter, thus attaining the same growth rate of the developing countries.[29] Five-year average annual growth rates for the period 1982–2014 are displayed in Table 1.2.

Similar to other emerging economies, Turkey has significantly benefitted from the remarkably favorable global liquidity environment in the period following 2001.[30] Reversal of these conditions in the global

*Table 1.2 Five-year average annual growth rates (1982–2014)*

| Periods | Average GDP growth rates |
|---------|--------------------------|
| 1982–1986 | 5.3 |
| 1987–1991 | 4.3 |
| 1992–1996 | 4.4 |
| 1997–2001 | 1.5 |
| 2002–2006 | 7.2 |
| 2007–2014 | 3.4 |

*Source:* Undersecretariat of Treasury.[31]

economy with the global financial crisis of 2008–2009 paved the way to the observed slowdown in the economy. This was further aggravated by the policy choices of the government to slow down the economy in order to deal with the large current account deficit. Economic growth in 2014 has been 2.9 percent, and the GDP reached 800 billion USD at current prices. Although the country achieved a rate slightly above the average GDP growth rate of emerging countries, which was 2.7 percent, this achievement was below the official goal of 3.3 percent.[32]

Turkey has challenging targets in relation to its vision for 2023, the 100th anniversary of the establishment of the Republic. The ruling Justice and Development Party (AKP) aims to become the 10th largest economy with a GDP of 2 trillion USD and a per capita income of 25,000 USD.[33] Targets of the government seem to be ambitious and unattainable in the light of the predictions of the international community. Goldman Sachs predicted that Turkey would stagnate and become the 16th largest economy in 2015. Its performance has been relatively worse than expected, and it was ranked the 18th largest economy in spite of its 4 percent growth[34] in 2015. OECD's prediction for 2060 for Turkey is that it would be the 12th largest economy in the world.

## Stock Market Capitalization

Turkey's experience with the stock exchange is relatively new. The stock exchange was established in 1986 within the framework of the Capital Market Law enacted in 1981 as a part of financial liberalization program. At the first year of its operation, there were 42 listed companies in the Istanbul Stock Exchange (ISE), with a total market capitalization of 938 million USD as of the end of 1986.[35] Development of the stock exchange was slow in its first three years, reaching 50 listed companies, with a market capitalization of 6.8 billion USD, corresponding to 6.3 percent of the GDP of Turkey. The number of listed companies increased to 110 with an upsurge of Initial Public Offerings (IPOs) in 1990, market capitalization reaching to 19.1 billion USD, corresponding to 12.7 percent of the GDP. With an uneven pace of increase, the number of publicly-listed companies has reached 405. Market capitalization of these listed companies was 308.8 billion USD in 2012,

amounting to the 39.1 percent of the country's GDP. While the number
of listed companies decreased slightly to 392 by the end of 2014, market
capitalization dropped down to 188.9 billion USD, corresponding to
27.5 percent of the GDP.[36]

The number of listed companies and their market capitalization both
as billion USD and as percent of GDP are presented in Table 1.3.

*Table 1.3 Stock market capitalization of the Istanbul Stock Exchange (1990–2012)*

| Years | Number of listed companies | Market capitalization (billion USD-current) | Market capitalization (% of GDP) |
|---|---|---|---|
| 1990 | 110 | 19.1 | 12.7 |
| 1991 | 134 | 15.7 | 10.4 |
| 1992 | 145 | 9.9 | 6.2 |
| 1993 | 152 | 37.5 | 20.8 |
| 1994 | 176 | 21.6 | 16.5 |
| 1995 | 205 | 20.8 | 12.3 |
| 1996 | 228 | 30.0 | 16.5 |
| 1997 | 258 | 61.1 | 32.2 |
| 1998 | 277 | 33.6 | 12.5 |
| 1999 | 285 | 112.7 | 45.1 |
| 2000 | 315 | 69.7 | 26.1 |
| 2001 | 310 | 47.1 | 24.1 |
| 2002 | 288 | 34.0 | 14.6 |
| 2003 | 284 | 68.4 | 22.6 |
| 2004 | 296 | 98.3 | 25.1 |
| 2005 | 302 | 161.5 | 33.4 |
| 2006 | 314 | 162.4 | 30.6 |
| 2007 | 319 | 286.6 | 44.3 |
| 2008 | 317 | 117.9 | 16.1 |
| 2009 | 315 | 225.7 | 36.7 |
| 2010 | 337 | 306.7 | 41.9 |
| 2011 | 362 | 201.8 | 26.0 |
| 2012 | 405 | 308.8 | 39.1 |

Data are extracted from the World Bank Global Development Indicators.[37]

Despite the efforts of related institutions to encourage companies to raise funds from the stock market, the role of the stock market in the economy remains relatively modest.

Furthermore, there seems to be a concentration in the stock market, large family groups and financial institutions, especially banks, with a relatively high share of the total market capitalization of the Borsa İstanbul, previously named the ISE. Koç Holding and the Sabancı Holding are the two oldest and largest family business groups in Turkey. Listed companies of these two business groups, specifically the Koç Holding with its eight listed companies and the Sabancı Holding with its 10 listed companies, constitute more than one-fourth of the total market capitalization in the Borsa Istanbul as of 2014.[38]

Banks are the predominant financial institutions of the business context in Turkey. Hence, they are the major providers of finance for production activities, being involved in servicing of public debt requirements, and conducting a wide array of financial transactions.[39] The economy is thus bank-based, and the role of the stock market in national economy is therefore limited.

## Public versus Privately Held Companies

The Turkish economic landscape is heavily dominated by small and medium-sized enterprises (SMEs) with a low share of large companies. SMEs constitute 99.9 percent of all enterprises; they provide 75.7 percent of jobs and produce 52.9 percent of all value-added in the economy, according to the statistics in 2011.[40] There are 3,506 companies categorized as large companies, and their share in the total number of companies is only 0.1 percent. An overwhelming majority of these large companies is privately held.

In their study, Gönenç et al.[41] identify five different types of enterprises in the Turkish business context: "Micro businesses, small- and medium-sized businesses, large family firms, institutional corporations and skilled stars." These categories differ in terms of their human and physical capital inputs, management quality, formalization, and transparency, and their level of access to product, capital, and labor markets. Categorized as "institutional corporations," publicly held companies include family business group of companies, formerly state-owned companies privatized through IPOs, and international companies operating in Turkey. There are 383 companies trading in the Borsa İstanbul, 38 of which are financial institutions and banks. "Institutional companies" constitute a small share in the business sector. Their share in total business sector employment is about four percent, while their share in total manufacturing employment is around six percent. Despite having a small share, they rank at the highest level with respect to institutionalization, productivity, and salaries of their employees. Publicly held companies satisfy the corporate governance and transparency requirements of the Borsa İstanbul and the regulatory authority, the Capital Market Board (CMB). These demanding and regulatory requirements of the market together with the relatively rigid labor laws and regulations of the business context might be decreasing the competitive strength of the publicly held companies in the international markets,[42] thereby displaying the reluctance of companies in going public.

Companies seem reluctant to offer their shares to public. In the largest 500 industrial companies list compiled in 2014, there are only 80 companies trading in the stock exchange, Borsa İstanbul.[43] Furthermore, this is displaying a decreasing trend, as the same number was 90 in 2009.[44] Characteristics of the current legislative and regulatory environment and the resulting need of the owners to maintain control over their companies are among possible reasons for the observed reluctance in going public. Besides, owners' perceptions about unfavorable business prospects after the IPO seem to hinder companies from going public. Owners have additional concerns in going public over increased costs of compliance with the transparency and corporate governance requirements, slowdown in their business processes due to increased supervision and artificial movements in the prices of their shares of stocks in the market.[45]

The number of companies going public and the amount of proceeds from IPOs has displayed an irregular pattern since the establishment of the Borsa İstanbul, formerly the ISE, which was established in 1986. While the market has witnessed increased IPO activity in some years, such as in 1990 and 2000, the IPO market remained relatively inactive in certain years.[46] The number of companies going public has remained limited in the years following the financial crisis of 2001, though proceeds from IPOs have been relatively high in some of these years, for instance in 2005, 2006, and 2008, as a result of IPOs of the privatizations of two large state banks and the Turkish Telekom, the leading state-owned telecommunications company.[47] In order to revive the IPO market, a protocol was signed by the ISE and CMB of Turkey in 2008 in an attempt to start an IPO campaign and encourage companies to go public. The campaign has succeeded in generating some activity in the IPO market, where 19 companies went public and generated total IPO proceeds of 1,218 billion USD in 2010; yet, IPO activity remained generally modest in the following years. The Borsa İstanbul continued its campaign for encouraging companies to offer their shares to public by giving information to the owners of large companies all over Turkey. With this aim in mind, the Borsa İstanbul organized meetings with the chambers of commerce, chambers of industry, and other regional vocational associations. In addition, the top management team of the Borsa İstanbul targeted companies from various large company lists as potential IPO candidates, and visited owners and managers of these companies. The team conducted more than 500 company visits between September 2012 and July 2014 and reports an increased interest in IPO market by the owners and managers of these companies.[48] The process that companies go through in order to offer their shares to public is suggested to lead to an increased professionalism and institutionalization in the family owned businesses and to contribute to their sustainability by easing their succession from generation to generation.

## Global Competitiveness

The business environment in Turkey offers both opportunities and challenges for the private sector. In the last decade, the structural transformations of the country have been led by the dynamic private sector. The government generally implemented pro-business and pro-investment policies and undertook reforms to improve the regulatory environment for the businesses. Improvements in infrastructure and connectivity and urbanization policies have also contributed to the dynamism in the business sector.[49] In spite of notable achievements, the progress has recently stagnated and further improvements in the business context thus seem to be necessary to elevate the competitiveness of the economy. Quality of regulations is one of the areas influencing competitiveness. The World Bank report titled "Doing Business 2015"[50] ranks Turkey as 55th out of 189 countries with respect to its overall performance on the quality of its regulatory framework relating to the 11 areas in the life cycle of businesses, slipping four positions in this ranking from being the 51st country in 2014. The aggregate score of Turkey is 68.66 in 2015, which is slightly above its regional average of Europe and Central Asia. It ranks below Georgia, Bulgaria, and Romania, and above Ukraine and India in this regional category with respect to its overall performance. Considering the dimensions of regulatory quality score, the performance of the country is especially low in areas of "dealing with construction permits," "resolving insolvency," and "getting credits," with a ranking of 136th, 109th, and 89th, respectively. On the other hand, Turkey has had a relatively good performance on "protecting minority investors" and ranks 13th on this measure. "Getting electricity" and "enforcing contracts" are the other dimensions of this relatively good performance, where, among 189 countries, Turkey ranks 34th and 38th, respectively. On the dimension of "Starting a Business," Turkey ranks 79th in 2015 with respect to ease of starting a business, as it takes on average 7.0 procedures and 6.5 days to start a business and costs 16.4 percent of income per capita.[51] This performance represents a slight decline from 2014, when it took 6.0 procedures and 6.0 days to start a business and costed 12.7 percent of per capita income, as Turkey increased notary and registration fees to start a business. In summary, as compared to other countries in the region, it takes a shorter time to establish a business in Turkey, but it is relatively costlier. Consequently, business context with respect to regulatory framework includes both favorable prospects with respect to competitiveness and significant challenges.

The WEF takes a comprehensive approach in the assessment of competitiveness, evaluating the state of welfare and per capita income growth potential of economies through using the Global Competitiveness Index (GCI). This index is based on a comprehensive set of dimensions, grouped into 12 pillars: institutions, infrastructure, macroeconomic environment, health and primary education, higher education and training, goods market efficiency, labor market efficiency, financial market development, technological readiness, market size, business sophistication, and innovation.

In 2014–2015, Turkey ranked 45th out of 144 countries included in the study, with a GCI score of 4.46 out of a maximum score of 7.[52] Turkey made a considerable progress in the last decade from its 66th position in the list of 2004–2005;[53] however, continuing weaknesses still pose challenges for the competitiveness of the economy. Moreover, Turkey's performance substantially stagnated in the last three years, ranking the 43th and 44th in 2012–2013 and 2013–2014 listings, respectively. Turkey displays moderate performance on most of the pillars of competitiveness, with mixed indicators of performance within each of these indicators. One of the strong points of Turkey relates to the "market size" pillar, as it is ranked as the 16th economy considering the size of GDP as well as its domestic and foreign market size. Developments in "infrastructure" and "goods market efficiency" supported by improvements in the rules and norms of competition are also among other contributors to competitiveness. On the other hand, there are serious weaknesses of the economy limiting its competitive strength. "Labor market efficiency" is the weakest feature of the economy, as Turkey ranks 131th on this pillar. Rigidities of the labor market together with relatively low performance with respect to capacity to attract and retain talent, and share of women in the workforce also seem to hinder competitiveness. Institutions and the quality of education are the other areas posing challenges. Turkey has an overall score of 3.9 (out of 7) in the pillar of "institutions," with an especially low performance on judicial independence. Quality of primary education (rank 94), quality of management schools (rank 100), quality of math and science education (rank 98), extent of staff training (rank 91) are some of the dimensions in which Turkey lags behind.[54] The Human Development Report of the UN provides evidence supporting the WEF scores. Turkey ranks 69th, with an overall score of 0.759 in 2014,[55] which is slightly above the world average (median score of 0.0700). Moreover, it had the same ranking both in 2012 and 2013. These findings might suggest that economic developments are not fully reflected in human development of the country. In their comparative study exploring the relationship between competitiveness of a nation and its implications on human development, Ülengin et al.[56] assert that Turkey is "underutilizing its current competitiveness," though it has the potential to significantly increase its human development scores, including life expectancy at birth, combined gross enrollment score for primary, secondary, and tertiary schools and gross domestic product per capita, at a level beyond its current level of competitiveness.

According to GCI scores, another weakness of the economy is "innovation." Turkey seems to be behind its competitors with respect to innovation, especially in consideration of the low level of R&D spending of companies and capacity for innovation. Issues relating to human capital appear to be one of the most important drawbacks in restraining the competitive strength of the economy.

The financial crises of 1994 and 2000–2001, together with large fiscal deficits and the resulting inflationary pressures, have widely undermined the competitiveness of the economy.[57] The recurrent nature of the crises seems to suggest the continuing presence of institutional weaknesses.

The composition of the business sector also affects the competitiveness of the economy. Modern, professionally-managed companies constitute only a small portion, while micro-firms with unproductive business prospects make up the majority of the business sector. Furthermore, uneven compliance with laws and regulations and existence of unregistered economy put institutionalized and professionally-managed companies at a disadvantage and thus hinders their growth. Other salient problems hindering competitiveness relate to the tax system and rigidities of labor market regulation.[58]

## Imports & Exports

As mentioned before, the country moved from import substitution policy to export-oriented policy macroeconomic stabilization and financial liberalization program of January 1980. Although this corresponded to a period of growth in exports in most of the emerging countries, Turkey achieved the fastest growth rate in exports in the world in the decade following the liberalization program. Export volume has increased from 2.3 billion USD, and in 1979 to 12.9 billion USD in 1990. In terms of share of exports in GDP, this increase denotes a rise from 2.6 percent in 1979 to 8.6 percent in 1990.[59] Sectoral composition of exports also changed significantly during this period. The share of industrial products increased and constituted the majority of the exports in 1990, which was previously dominated by agricultural products.

As a percentage of GDP, export performance of Turkey stagnated during 1990s; however, the signing of a customs union with the EU in 1996 was a momentous landmark in the further liberalization of trade and integration with the European and the world economy. The Customs Union with the European Union significantly supported the acceleration in export growth and the increase in sophistication and diversification of exports observed in the 2000s. Turkey's export performance has been markedly strong after 2002. Between 2002 and 2012, Turkey achieved an annual growth rate of 16.5 percent in exports expressed in USD terms. This average annual growth rate is six percent above the rate of increase in global exports, comparable to the increase in exports in Brazil, Russia, and India.[60] In this period, exports increased in each of the years except for 2009, when exports decreased by 22.6 percent following the global economic recession. After 2012, export volume in USD mostly stayed constant in 2013, exhibiting a 0.4 percent decline and a modest increase of 3.8 percent, reaching USD 157.6 billion in 2014 (Table 1.4).[61]

*Table 1.4 Trade statistics*

|  | Exports (billion USD) | Imports (billion USD) | Trade deficit (billion USD) | Export to imports (%) |
|---|---|---|---|---|
| 2002 | 36.1 | 51.6 | −15.5 | 69.9 |
| 2003 | 47.3 | 69.3 | −22.1 | 68.1 |
| 2004 | 63.2 | 97.5 | −34.4 | 64.8 |
| 2005 | 73.5 | 116.8 | −43.3 | 62.9 |
| 2006 | 85.5 | 139.6 | −54.0 | 61.3 |
| 2007 | 103.7 | 170.1 | −62.8 | 63.1 |
| 2008 | 132.0 | 202.0 | −69.8 | 65.4 |
| 2009 | 102.1 | 140.9 | −38.8 | 72.5 |
| 2010 | 113.9 | 185.5 | −71.7 | 61.4 |
| 2011 | 134.9 | 240.8 | −105.9 | 56.0 |
| 2012 | 152.5 | 236.5 | −84.1 | 64.5 |
| 2013 | 151.8 | 251.7 | −99.9 | 60.3 |
| 2014 | 157.6 | 242.2 | −84.6 | 65.1 |

*Source:* TÜİK.[62]

Imports also remarkably increased between 2002 and 2012, thus widening the trade deficit. Displaying a fluctuating pattern, trade deficit increased from 15.1 billion in 2002 to 84.1 billion USD in 2012.[63] In 2013, imports were made up of manufactured products and fuels and mining products, constituting 57.9 and 25.1 percent of total import volume, respectively.

Between 2002 and 2012, Turkey diversified both its export composition and export markets. Its export performance depends on the developments in the manufacturing industry, as exports are mainly composed of manufactured goods.[64] The share of manufactured goods in exports is 76.1 percent as of 2013.[65] Manufactured goods have a high import component, indicating a high dependence of exports on imported intermediate products. The export component of the manufacturing industry also displayed an increasing trend during the end of this period. Additionally, product composition of exports changed in parallel to the structural developments in the manufacturing industry, which displayed a shift from traditional labor-intensive industries to capital-intensive industries, producing medium technology products. While exports of textiles and apparel dominated the exports in the beginning of this period, the shares of automotive sector, machinery, and metals also increased. Nevertheless, exports of high-technology products stagnated during the period, while some of the other emerging markets, such as China, Republic of Korea, Malaysia, India, and Poland, noticeably increased the shares of their exports of high-technology products.[66] Turkey was thus able to develop only a number of globally recognized brands, which are in low- and medium-technology industries, such as textiles, white goods products. Composition of the exports, with its reliance on medium-technology products, functioned as a factor limiting the export growth of the country as the global demand for medium-technology exports displayed modest increases during this period.[67]

Turkey also diversified its export markets after 2002. While it had 90 export markets in 2000, the number of countries that imported Turkish products increased to 137 at the end of 2012.[68] During this period, the European Union remained as the most prominent trading market, the share of exports to the European Union and European Free Trade Association (EFTA) region decreased, but the share to the Middle East and

North African (MENA) countries increased. As the demand from the EU countries declined after the global financial crisis of 2009, exporters experimented with new markets, especially in the MENA countries. The share of the European Union (28 countries) in total export volume was 42.3 percent in 2013, followed by the 7.9 percent share of Iraq.[69] The shares of the Russian Federation, the United States, and the United Arab Emirates were 4.6, 3.7, and 3.3 percent, respectively.

Export growth between 2002 and 2012 was attained mostly by the increases in the exports of existing exporters. New exporters entering the market were not quite successful. On the other hand, the period was also characterized by a high degree of both entry into and exit from the export markets. Thus the rate of survival of the new entrants to the export market in the long term was relatively low.[70] Most of the exports were generated by a small number of large companies, indicating a high degree of concentration in the market. In fact, top one percent of the exporters accounted for 60 percent of the exports in the period between 2002 and 2012,[71] while export performance of small and medium-sized companies remained relatively weak.[72]

Within the framework of the "Vision for 2023" for the 100th anniversary of the establishment of the Turkish Republic, the Ministry of Economy has coordinated the preparation of a strategic plan for the exports, mainly based on the aim of improving the competitiveness of the economy. The strategic plan titled "The Exports Strategy of Turkey for 2023" was approved by the Higher Planning Council in June 2012 and set a target of 500 billion USD of exports for 2023. This target corresponds to a pronounced increase over the level of exports in 2013, which were 151.8 billion USD. Reaching this target will require a considerable increase in the global market share of Turkey, almost doubling its share from 0.82 percent of global imports in 2012 to 1.46 percent in 2023. The plan includes a detailed road map including 19 strategic targets and performance indicators and 72 action plans envisioning a country that has accomplished its structural and technological transformation and has realized exports of high-value added and advanced technology products.[73] This vision will require further improvements and investments in infrastructure, human capital, and institutional framework.[74]

# Regional Trading Blocks

Situated between the east and the west both geographically and culturally, Turkey turned its face toward the west during the late Ottoman period and reinforced this orientation after the formation of the Republic. Turkey also broadened its scope, taking steps to establish relations and to strengthen its economic ties with the regional trading blocks, such as the Black Sea, the Central Asian Republics, and the countries from the Gulf and the Middle East.

The European Union is an important trading partner for Turkey. Bilateral trade between the European Union and Turkey has significantly increased after the signing of a customs union in 1996.[75] In the period between 1996 and 2011, trading volume with the European Union increased almost fourfold, reaching 58 billion USD in 2012. During the same periods, imports from the European Union tripled and Turkey thus became the sixth largest trading partner of the European Union; on the other hand, the European Union became the largest trading partner for Turkey as of 2012.[76] Customs Union with the European Union also contributed to an increase in foreign direct investments from the European Union. Countries from the European Union constitute the largest group of foreign investors in Turkey.[77] Turkey received a total of 81.7 billion USD foreign direct investments from the European Union in the period between 1996 and 2010.[78] Accession negotiations, starting after the official recognition of Turkey as a candidate country in 1999, still continue. The prospects of the country for joining European Union, however, seem to be low; moreover, businesses seem reluctant and uninterested about this issue.[79]

Turkey is a member of various multinational regional intergovernmental organizations, established with the aim of establishing cooperation on economic integration and trade. The Organization for Islamic Cooperation (OIC), the Economic Cooperation Organization (ECO), the Organization of the Black Sea Economic Cooperation (BSEC), and Developing 8 (D-8) are the Regional Initiatives[80] in which Turkey has participated. Countries from the Gulf and the Middle East comprise a recently emerging group of foreign investments, accounting for 12 percent of the foreign direct investment inflows in 2012.[81]

# CHAPTER 2

# Historical Background of Corporate Governance in Turkey

The history of a country has a significant overall impact on its institutional environment. Diverging historical forces have influenced the dominant business form, modes of enterprise creation, shareholder structure, and the relative role of different stakeholders in the Turkish context. Corporate governance, which has been open to Western influences since Ottoman times, has strived to accommodate them with local tradition and practices. Another historically embedded factor is the strong state tradition in Turkey. The latter had a significant impact on governance practices in both public and private sectors. Before reviewing the historical background of governance in Turkey, it may be useful to have a quick look at the major historically embedded characteristics such as language and religion.

## Languages Spoken; Religious Adherence

Turkish is the official language in the country. A poll conducted by KONDA in 2007 on native languages in Turkey shows that 85.54 percent of the population speaks Turkish, and 12.98 percent different dialects of Kurdish. In recent years, 2.7 million Syrian refugees have migrated to Turkey,[1] which thus indicates that a sizeable portion of the population now speaks Arabic.

According to official estimates, 99 percent of the population is Muslim, with Hanafi Sunnis constituting the largest group among them. Alevis, the disciples of a belief system combining facets of both Shia and Sunni Islam and the traditions of other religious groups indigenous to the region, make up the second largest group.[2] The remaining one percent comprises the following religious identities:[3] Jews, Greek Orthodox Christians, Armenian Orthodox Christians (citizens + recent undocumented immigrants from Armenia), Roman Catholics (mostly recent immigrants from Africa and Philippines), Syrian Orthodox Christians (Suryanis), Russian Orthodox Christians (mostly recent immigrants from Russia with resident permits), Bahais, Yezidis, Jehova's Witnesses, Iraqi Chaldean Christians, Bulgarian Orthodox, Nestorian, Georgian Orthodox, other Protestant Christians, Syrian Catholic Christians, Armenian Catholic Christians, Maronite Christians, and Atheists. Although the Turkish state is legally secular, the Turkish Muslim community is one of the most religious ones in Europe.[4] In a recent study,[5] it is observed that two-third of the population prioritize his/her Muslim identity over the Turkish one, while three out of four people are "very proud" of their Turkish identity.

## Historical Influences

The strong state tradition has long been a major characteristic of Turkish communities where state is initially perceived as a sacred reflection of the cosmic order created by God.[6] The central state tradition has always been very influential in previous Turkish communities (like the early ones in Central Asia and later in Anatolia) as well as in the current Turkish republic. This centrality of the state has a strong molding effect on the business system as well as on the corporate governance practices and the underlying legal infrastructure. Briefly stated, "the authoritative role and monopolistic place of the state at the expense of the individual actors" has always shaped the social domain[7] and the business system. During the reforms carried out throughout the 19th century, the French civil law, which was in line with this cultural background, was adopted by the Ottoman Empire.[8] This further led to the centralized distribution of resources by the state. The passage from the Ottoman Empire to the Turkish Republic witnessed a continuity in this direction. Turkey has a patrimonial state tradition in the sense that the state supplies jobs for lower income strata and provides subsidies to "eligible" businesspeople through a rather "discretionary and discriminatory process with frequently changing rules."[9] This also makes high-level uncertainty a major characteristic of the business environment in the country. Private sector is very much dependent on state allocations. Close interactions with the government, thus nonmarket strategies, become increasingly more important than market strategies for businesspeople interested more in maintaining good relations with the political elites and bureaucrats than in finding an equilibrium of supply and demand.[10] Frequent policy changes and interventions of the state further increase this level of severe unpredictability. This situation of state-induced uncertainty explains the paradoxical stance of Turkey in terms of its corporate governance laws and their implementation. Despite the existence of laws regulating the governance, the will to put them into force is visibly limited.

A retrospective overview of the developments in the domain of corporate governance may be helpful to assess the current conception of governance. This necessitates a closer look on the acquisition of property rights and the early forms of businesses during the Ottoman period, preceding the current Turkish Republic that inherited many institutions from the former. In the Ottoman Empire, private property was inexistent until 1858, with only some exceptions,[11] an absence that acted as a barrier in the accumulation of capital and thus in the creation of related institutions. State has always retained the focal role in the economy and in the distribution of privileges,[12] thereby encouraging selected families to become entrepreneurs.

Following a free trade agreement that was signed in 1838, first with Britain then expanded to include other European countries,[13] the Ottoman Empire adopted a decisive move toward westernization in 1839 with the proclamation of the Tanzimat, literally meaning "reorganization." The international scope of business transactions considerably increased. The pressures inducing changes in the commercial legal infrastructure originated from developed capitalist countries rather than from internal local constituencies.[14] In the eyes of companies from developed countries, the Ottoman Empire was a market to sell their products, which were much more competitively priced due to their increased industrialization. The Ottoman Empire was also a source of inexpensive raw materials; and foreign companies invested in the Ottoman territory for their supplies.[15] International investors, therefore, insisted for a change in the legal system. As a corollary consequence, the ministry of trade and commercial courts were established in 1839.[16]

In 1839, Mahmut II established the Ministry of Trade by adopting the model of some European countries[17] with the purpose of developing commerce, agriculture, and industry, and centralizing the activities in these domains. The commercial revolution of the 18th century led way to complex commercial transactions, which had been difficult to handle within the restricted scope of the existing religious laws and courts[18] of the Ottoman Empire. Newly established nonreligious courts dealt with commercial issues, obligations, and administrative law. Although the jurisdiction domain of the Islamic courts was limited, the religious courts along with the nonreligious ones coexisted, which thus created a dual legal system.[19] The dual legal structure with religious and nonreligious laws and courts was abolished after the adoption of the unified Western laws following the proclamation of the Turkish republic in 1923.

The late period of Ottoman rule was also characterized by attempts to grow and to internationalize the business and companies by organizing international exhibitions (in 1863) and encouraging small firms to get together with similar others to combine their forces.[20] Bank-i Dersaadet (Bank of Constantinople), the first institution bearing the name of "bank," was set up in 1846.[21] That was followed in 1863 by the establishment of "Bank-ı Osmani-i Şahane" (the Imperial Ottoman Bank) by British and French investors. The bank augmented its power over the Ottoman rulers by acquiring the right to issue currency.

As previously mentioned, the state has always had a central position in the Turkish business system, thus having the capacity to introduce new forms of companies into the system. One of those was the Şirket-i Hayriye (the Bosphorus Steamboat Company) founded in 1851 with the initiatives of two state officials of the Ottoman Empire, namely Fuat Pasha and Cevdet Pasha. Having seen the steam boats during their stay in Bucharest, they promoted the idea that steam boats could be useful for travels over the Bosphorus and presented their proposal to the authorities. This was the first local corporation ("anonim şirket" in Turkish) whose capital was divided into shares.[22] Even though the company started its operations in 1854, its first-known statute dates back to 1872 where there was no mention of the capital of the company and the statute covered limited number of areas.[23] The shareholders of the company were state officials and Ottoman imperial family members, including the Sultan himself. This was made on purpose to attract local people and to convince them to become shareholders. As a matter of fact, the corporation "anonim şirket" was used by the government as a tool to create investors among local people and to increase wealth through business.[24] However, there was limited success in attracting local people. Consequently, some bankers such as Camondo and dealers of gold in Galata were invited to become shareholders of the company.[25]

Following the introduction of the Commercial Law in 1850, which consisted of the translation of the two sections of French Commercial Law of 1807,[26] the French law was thus once again copied in 1863 (enhanced with the laws of other countries) to create Ottoman maritime trade clauses regulating the trade practices in this specific area.

The adoption of new laws was a clear shift from the religious law for the trade issues that had been poorly covered in the very much scattered religious rules and regulations. There was a multiplicity of legal systems (such as courts for foreigners by the consulates, religious courts for the Muslim community, etc.), which in turn were leading to contradictions, complexities, and redundancies in the search of justice.[27] For example, the religious law envisaged only one type of company, which was far from fulfilling the requirements and needs of business activities. The new Commercial Law included various types of businesses. However, the latter was almost limited to the classifications of companies ("kollektif," "komandit," "anonim"), and this limited scope necessitated further amendments over the years.[28] For instance, provisions about bankruptcy, insurance, and checks were added, respectively, in 1905, 1906, and 1914.[29]

The statutes of the companies were also adopted from the Western countries. These were originally in French and were then used by the Turkish state again acting as an example. The statutes started to be drafted in Turkish during the "national firm" movement after 1908.[30] The first model statute for corporations ("anonim şirket") appeared in 1882, though it had previously been used by the state. Each part of the statutes included various facets of governance that were as follows:[31] The first part of the statute comprised "the memorandum of association, the name of the company, and the location of the registered office." The second part included the aim of the company and its activity domains. The third part contained the information in relation to the formation of the capital, the state of the shares, installments, the proportion, and the form of capital increase. The fourth part consisted of the internal administration of the company, the board of directors, the selection of its members, the length of their period of duty, conditions for selection, the duties and the responsibilities of the board, the frequency of meeting, the salaries, and the fees of the members. The fifth part covered rules about the functioning of the general council, the conditions for member selection, the authority and responsibilities of the council, frequency of the meetings, and decision-making rules. While the sixth section covered the important dates for the financial year and the inspection of the accounts, the seventh contained the clauses related to the distribution of the profits. As for the eighth part, it incorporated the conditions and the limit of transfers from annual profits to the extraordinary expenditures. The ninth part comprised conditions for the changes in the statutes. And the final part explained the conditions for liquidations and mergers.

According to stock exchange regulations, in order to exchange shares and bonds the companies were required to be quoted to Istanbul Stock Exchange[32] that was opened in 1866[33] during the Ottoman rule. Following the second constitutional period, which started in 1908, new incentives to encourage investments were adopted. This was a period of transition to both political and economic liberalism in which private investment and foreign investors were encouraged.[34] The increasing number and types of companies necessitated changes in the model statutes that Akyıldız explained as follows:[35]

The restrictions concerning the location of the head office, the number of board members, the number of directors to be changed each year, and the frequency of board meetings were all lifted. In the new statutes, the founders were asked to fill in the names of the directors of the first board. Similarly, the companies were required to inform the Ministry at least 20 days before any meetings of the general assembly where a police superintendent appointed by the ministry should be present. All the reports (of the board and the inspectors), minutes of the assembly, ledgers with the names of the participants, and their shares as well as balance sheet of the company were required to be submitted to the Ministry of

Trade. Furthermore, companies were asked to publish their statutes in the newspapers no later than one month after receiving the foundation permission from the government. They were also asked to announce in a similar way the changes in the statutes, the decisions of the general assembly, and their balance sheet. The shares were also required to provide information about the company's aims and scope of operations, its capital and owners, conditions of capital increase, and profit distribution.

Another novelty in this period was a decree by the Sultan Mehmet Reşat, which impeded any member of the Ottoman dynasty to become a board member or chairperson in corporations. This was an attempt to prevent unfair competition of the firms as well as to protect the reputation of the Ottoman dynasty. Companies were also recognized as corporate bodies and were given the right to own land in 1913.

Hence, the initial legal framework for the organization of the corporations and different types of companies were put into force during the last years of the Ottoman Empire. Although the implementation of the 1850 Commercial Law was limited, it set the initial guidelines for the creation of different types of business and initial rules for governance.

The Ottoman Empire collapsed following World War I and the Turkish Republic was founded in 1923 following an independence war. The Ottoman Empire that preceded the Turkish Republic can be defined as a semi-colonial society, especially in its last years, where industrialization attempts were obstructed by the expansion of capitulations dating back to the 1838 Baltalimanı Anglo-Turkish Commercial Convention.[36,37]

Number of industrial firms may give an idea about the economic conditions prevailing in the Ottoman Empire right before its collapse. From 1913 to 1915, there were only 264 industrial establishments with more than 10 workers, which operated predominantly in textiles, food processing, paper and printing, and timber;[38] and by the late 1920s, there were around 130 significant industrial establishments in the country.[39,40] Therefore, since its early days, the new Turkish Republic gave priority to the development of local industry by adopting a law for the encouragement of industry in 1927.[41] For this purpose, the local investors were visited by the government officials and even by the head of the Republic, Mustafa Kemal Atatürk, and were invited to start new ventures in different areas. The president himself also took the lead to establish the İş Bankası (the

"Business Bank"), which was financed by private capital[42,43] and aimed at supporting new investments through participations or credit allocations. Given the impact of the Great Depression in 1929, the private sector development could not reach the targets set initially. This gave way to a Soviet-type planned economic development in mid-1930s and to the establishment of the state-owned enterprises.[44]

Single party politics characterized Turkish political life until 1946. Therefore, the Republican People's Party (Cumhuriyet Halk Partisi— CHP) that was created by a military-bureaucratic elite reigned until 1950. The public and, to a certain degree, the private sector prospered during this period, although there were also some moments of antagonism between the state and the latter. An important example was the case of the new Wealth Tax Act in 1942 targeting mainly minority business owners. Following the adoption of the tax, a predominantly "Muslimized entrepreneurship potential" moved into the industrial sector.[45] The businesses of minority businessmen failing to pay the tax were taken over by Muslim entrepreneurs. After 1950, the Democratic Party that newly came into power, adopted a pro-business economic policy resulting in a considerable increase in the number of joint stock and limited companies.[46,47] Businesses prospered during this period, which was also characterized by an opening to foreign investors through the Law for Encouragement of Foreign Investment, which "induced industry to be one consisting of reassembling imported parts."[48]

Following the military coup in 1960, economic policy shifted to planned economy through five-year-plans with components as import substitution and protectionism.[49] The latter accompanied with high inflation rate contributed to the significant growth of businesses and TÜSİAD (Türk Sanayicileri ve İşadamları Derneği—Turkish Association of Industrialists and Businessmen) was established in the early 1970s. Economic instability and high inflation of 1970s were handled by a "shock therapy";[50] and in 1980, import substitution policy was abandoned, coupled with the adoption of export-led industrial policy with the encouragement of the International Monetary Fund (IMF) and the World Bank.[51]

Liberalization and internationalization of the economy brought about privatization of state economic enterprises and the abandoning of mixed economy characterized by a heavy protectionist and national tone. Significant developments such as the foundation of Istanbul Stock Exchange (ISE—now Borsa İstanbul), the abandoning of the control on foreign currency, the determination of the value of the Turkish Lira in the market, the suppression of foreign capital entry controls followed. Early 1980s were also characterized by significant efforts to bring together Islamic identity and liberal economy, which further increased with the triumph of pro-Islamist parties in the 1990s and 2000s.[52] This also resulted in the emergence of business networks with religious tones such as the MÜSİAD (Müstakil Sanayici ve İşadamları Derneği—The Association of Independent Industrialists and Businesspeople) and TUSKON (Türkiye İşadamları ve Sanayiciler Konfederasyonu—The Confederation of Turkish Businesspeople and Industrialists).

## Major CG Legislation After the Creation of the New Turkish State

The new Turkish state created its national assembly in 1920 and proclaimed the republic in 1923. Even during the early years of the young Turkish government in Ankara, the attempts to create large companies and a proper governance framework were carried on. For example, the Turkish National Import and Export Company was established as a corporation with the initiative and encouragement of the Ministry of Economy in 1922 in Ankara[53] (after the establishment of the National Assembly in 1920, but before the proclamation of the republic in 1923). Among the shareholders, there were 54 deputies of the national assembly and 37 merchants; besides, the company issued stocks for one lira and publicized heavily to attract large numbers of people.[54] The advertisement stressed that anyone could be a founding member and that there were clauses in the statutes to inhibit the domination of the large shareholders.[55] These may be considered as early discussions on corporate governance in the Republican Turkey.

The types of the companies further diversified with the new adjustments in the laws in later years. The first holding company after the proclamation of the Republic appears to be the Yatırımlar Holding (Investments Holding), which was established by a decree issued after the military coup in May 27, 1960.[56] This was followed by the establishment in 1963 of the Koç Holding, which is actually the largest corporation in Turkey. This move of the Koç Holding seems to be an example followed by other major corporations such as the Sabancı Group.

The legal structure of the country underwent a pronounced westernization after the proclamation of the Republic in 1923. The new Turkish Commercial Code prepared by taking into consideration various countries laws[57] (especially German and Italian laws) was put into force in 1926.[58] On the other hand, the new civil law was based on the Swiss Federal Code in 1926 and the property and inheritance rights were secured with the new constitution of 1924.[59] The Ministry of Labor was established in 1945 to regulate labor relations. The Turkish Commercial Code underwent changes first in 1957 and finally in 2012. The company law provisions of the previous commercial code of 1957 on joint stock companies and on limited liability companies were adapted from the Swiss company law.[60]

Major changes in corporate governance took place after the policy shift to liberalization in 1980 in harmony with the global trend. Corporate governance is structured by the Turkish Commercial Code; the Capital Market Law; and the regulations by the Capital Markets Board (CMB) of Turkey along with the specific laws for banking and telecommunications sectors.[61] The CMB was empowered by the Capital Market Law (CML) in 1981. It regulates the capital markets, supervises the compliance with the legislation, takes precaution to prevent breaches, and finally instigates sanctions in case there is a breach of law.[62] Its mission statement is declared in its website as the following:[63]

> To make innovative regulations, and to perform supervision with the aim of ensuring fairness, efficiency and transparency in Turkish capital markets, and improving their international competitiveness.

In 1986, the ISE was opened. And in 1989, the Turkey Fund started to operate in order to attract foreign capital to Turkey.[64] Following the 1980 military coup, which eased the transition to liberalization policy induced by the international financial community (containing different international finance institutions), the attempts of integration with international markets gained momentum.[65] Starting from 1980, a series of laws were passed through which the limits on foreign exchange rate, foreign control of domestic assets were lifted, and foreign investors could invest in company stocks in the ISE. In spite of all the efforts to create a market-based system after 1980, the Turkish system continued to be bank-based mainly due to the fact that the banks had relatively diversified portfolio of activities such as traditional depository functions and investment banking in a periphery context with a historically weak capital market.[66] Laws passed after 1980 allowed banks to release their own securities and to act as intermediaries in capital markets, enabling them to hand over 90 percent of securities in the ISE by mid-1990s.[67] The Banking Law was revised in 1999 and several amendments were made following the 2001 banking crisis. The amendments included important clauses in terms of the governance. Another banking law adapted to the EU legislation was passed in 2005.

In line with the liberalization movement, several other institutions were founded, namely the Competition Authority (1994), the Banking Regulation and Supervision Agency (1999), the Telecommunication Authority (2000), the Energy Market Regulatory Board (2001); and new laws such as the new Turkish Court of Accounts were enacted, thus influencing governance practices at the public and private sectors.[68]

Turkey's EU candidacy and the resulting process of adaptation to the EU law introduced substantial revisions into the codes, including the Turkish Commercial Code,[69] the Competition Law (2008), and the new Capital Market Law (2012). In fact, the new Turkish Corporate Code was approved as of January 13, 2011 by the Parliament and became effective on July 1, 2012, while some of its parts were only implemented in 2013. The new code made substantial changes in corporate governance, capital maintenance, disclosure, and independent audit.[70] It covers areas such as the qualifications for board membership, minority rights protection, establishment of proxy voting and electronic voting principles, permission for online general meetings via websites, specification of the minimum informational content required in annual reports and company websites, and the prerequisite regarding the auditors to be independent audit firms or certified public accountants.[71] It also makes possible the formation of a corporation with a sole shareholder and eventually a board with a sole director.

## Major Corporate Scandals

According to the Global Competitiveness Index, Turkey ranks 45th with a score of 4.46 over 7 among 144 countries.[72] The score of private institutions regarding corporate ethics is 4 over 7 and in this regard, Turkey ranks 68th among 144 countries.[73] Even though listed companies seem to be aware of the corporate compliance standards, Turkish companies do not adopt compliance programs unless they are quoted in multiple stock exchanges or they launch a business with a foreign partner.[74] Nonlisted companies and small and medium-sized enterprises (SMEs) seem to have less exposure to compliance programs and internal controls.[75]

The Phase 3 Report on implementing OECD convention on anti-bribery in Turkey states that business organizations such as the Turkish Contractors Associations (TCA) and the TÜSİAD have a sound understanding of corporate compliance programs and internal controls.[76] The report mentions that many members of both organizations were actively involved in the Global Compact and Global Ethics Network. Both have been active in publishing codes of ethics or road map to ethical business. However, major institutions such as the TCAs and the Foreign Economic Relations Board do not mention bribery or internal control mechanisms as headings in their documents. According to the same report, government agencies seem to be less active than businesses in promoting awareness on internal controls and compliance programs. The highly politicized nature of government agencies and state enterprises is a significant constraint on the adoption of responsible governance practices in those institutions. On the other hand, Turkey ranks 66th with a score of 42 over 100, according to the Transparency International's 2015 Corruption Perceptions Index measuring the public sector corruption in 168 countries.[77] The Transparency International identifies "low and inconsistent levels of access to information, ineffective application of asset disclosure requirements, absent or unimplemented codes of conduct, political interference in institutional responsibilities and operations and poor working conditions for judges, legislative staff and civil servants" as major problems areas.[78] This relatively poor and discriminatory supervisory scope of the institutional environment may be one of the leading factors behind the corporate scandals.

Especially after the liberalization in 1980, corporate scandals occurred in the financial sector, which was the first to be deregulated. The beginning of 2000s was another marking period in terms of the scandals in the financial sector. The general definition of finance capital as the scope where industry and banks combine interests under the dominance of banks does not hold true in the Turkish context where "industrial and commercial-based holding groups subordinate the banks' operations to the groups' overall interests."[79] The 1958 Banking Act targeted to stabilize and to increase domestic credit supplies and permitted banks whose shares (at least 25 percent) were held within large Turkish holding groups to provide unlimited funds to their affiliated companies thus, to their shareholders.[80] This law opened up the way to an irresponsible use of bank assets against the interest of other stakeholders. In 2000, loose licensing criteria, controlling families with no or limited sector experience and aiming only to fund their own investments in various sectors combined with the "corrosive role played in the market" by the state-owned banks acting in line with the will of the government (even bypassing the laws) resulted in a series of bank scandals.[81] A total of 22 banks were taken over by the banking supervisory authority. This led to a total restructuring of the legal framework concerning the banking sector after 2001, which later successfully survived the 2008 global financial crises. However, the move toward a rule-based governance is still not complete, and nowadays it is contested in many instances.[82] Corporate scandals have been frequent in the financial sector among the state-owned companies as well. For example, the Emlakbank, which was established as a state bank in 1926 with the objective of providing home mortgages and real estate funds, was subject to politicized governance practices with frequent changes in the upper echelon, overstaffing and opaque credit allocations, and finally was transferred to the Banking Supervisory Authority in 2001.[83]

Absence of an effective capital market in Turkey has driven searches for alternative forms of capitalization, thus, leading to an emergence of multi-ownership companies as an alternative model.[84] Since 1960s, small investors such as Turkish workers in foreign countries or people with limited savings in periphery cities in Anatolia put their savings in new or existing holding companies with a prospect of good returns. However, these holding companies often failed and their activities resulted in abuses

due to the absence of supporting regulatory schemes and lack of institutional bases of impersonal trust mechanisms in the economy. "Populist
politics, lax oversight, social norms that incorporate gambling" have long
been the factors behind the failure of creating effective capital markets[85]
and related governance mechanisms.

Furthermore, corporate scandals also continued at an increasing pace
during the last decade. One well-known example is the case of the major
mobile operator in Turkey, Turkcell, which was established in 1994 (see
www.turkcell.com for further details). The company is co-founded by one
of the wealthiest businessmen, Mehmet Emin Karamehmet, owning also
the Çukurova Family Business Group. It is listed in both the New York
Stock Exchange and Borsa İstanbul since 2000. Family-owned Çukurova
Group wants to keep control of the company against two large shareholders, namely TeliaSonera (a Nordic telecoms operator) and Altimo,
(affiliated with a large investment company Alfa Group).[86] Initially,
the Çukurova Group and TeliaSonera respectively possessed 52.91 and
47.09 percent of the shares in the Turkcell Holding, which in turn owned
51 percent of the shares in Turkcell. During a period when the Çukurova
Holding experienced a crisis of cash flow, the Çukurova and TeliaSonera
entered into a letter agreement concerning the potential sale of Çukurova's shares in Turkcell Holding to TeliaSonera,[87] which would then allow
the latter to control the company. Following a higher offer from Altimo,
the agreement was suspended by the Çukurova Holding, and the Share
Purchase Agreement (SPA) was not signed within the period specified in
the letter agreement. TeliaSonera brought the dispute to the international
court of arbitration. The tribunal decided in 2011 that Çukurova was
liable to pay compensation to TeliaSonera in the sum of $932 million.[88]
Since 2005, the ongoing conflict over the ownership of the company in
various courts dramatically influenced its corporate governance practices
concerning dividend distribution, general assembly meetings, board and
top management team staffing. For instance, the partners could not reach
a consensus over the selection of the independent directors. Following
this conflict, the Turkcell Holding (51 percent of the shares) decided
not to be present at the general shareholders meeting, which resulted
in the annulment of the latter. The rights of the minority shareholders

were thus damaged, and they called for government intervention. For instance, an announcement made by Turkcell to the Public Disclosure Platform (KAP—Kamuyu Aydınlatma Platformu) indicates that the general assembly meetings for the years 2010–2011–2012–2013–2014, which were blocked by the partners, could only be organized on March 26, 2015.[89] Only then the decisions about the submittal and approval of board members, dividends for the years 2010–2011–2012 and 2013, and other major issues such as profit and loss statements, auditing were finally discussed. Consequently, governance-related decisions for the years 2010–2011–2012–2013–2014 were taken all at once at the General Meeting held in 2015. The agenda of the meeting presented in Table 2.1 displays the extent of violation of governance rules between 2010 and 2014. (The emphasis in bold on past years was added by the authors of the book.)

The story does not end there either. To retrieve its shares, the Çukurova Group obtained credit from a state bank, Ziraat Bankası (literally meaning, the Agricultural Bank), which led the way to the nomination of state officials close to the AKP government to the board and to some important positions in the company.[90] In 2014, four top executives including the CEO resigned. The executive positions have been increasingly staffed with managers close to government, and huge amounts of spending have been diverted to businesses and media outlets close to the government.[91]

While some of the corporate scandals in the private sector originate from the misbehavior of the owners, others stem from the weak property rights and the strong position of government in the Turkish context. Discretionary and discriminatory processes with frequently changing rules render the Turkish business environment uncertain in terms of governance. For example, in several instances, state intervention created serious governance problems against the interests and rights of the stakeholders including shareholders. In the media sector, government's strong pressure on business owners to sell their businesses, which are subsequently handed over to the businessmen supporting the government, poses a serious threat to transparency and fairness principles of the governance (see the part on news media).

*Table 2.1 The agenda of the annual general assembly meeting of Turkcell*

| TURKCELL İLETİŞİM HİZMETLERİ A.Ş. |
| --- |
| AGENDA OF THE ANNUAL GENERAL ASSEMBLY MEETING OF THE YEARS |
| 2010, 2011, 2012, 2013, and 2014 |

1. Opening and election of the Presidency Board;
2. Authorizing the Presidency Board to sign the minutes of the meeting;
3. Reading the Annual Report of the Board of Directors relating to the fiscal year 2010;
4. Reading the Statutory Auditors' Report relating to the fiscal year 2010;
5. Reading the summary of the Independent Audit Firm's Report relating to the fiscal year 2010;
6. Reading, discussion, and approval of the Balance Sheets and Profits/Loss statements relating to the fiscal year 2010;
7. Discussion of and decision on the distribution of dividend for the year 2010 and determination of the dividend distribution date;
8. Release of the board member, Colin J. Williams, from activities and operations of the Company pertaining to the year 2010;
9. Release of the Statutory Auditors individually from activities and operations of the Company pertaining to the year 2010;
10. Reading the Annual Report of the Board of Directors relating to the fiscal year 2011;
11. Reading the Statutory Auditors' Report relating to the fiscal year 2011;
12. Reading the summary of the Independent Audit Firm's Report relating to the fiscal year of 2011;
13. Reading, discussion, and approval of the Balance Sheets and Profits/Loss statements relating to the fiscal year 2011;
14. Discussion of and decision on the distribution of dividend for the year 2011 and determination of the dividend distribution date;
15. Release of the Board members individually from the activities and operations of the Company pertaining to the year 2011;
16. Release of the Statutory Auditors individually from activities and operations of the Company pertaining to the year 2011;
17. Reading the Annual Report of the Board of Directors relating to fiscal year 2012;
18. Reading the Statutory Auditors' Report relating to fiscal year 2012;
19. Discussion of and approval of the election of the independent audit firm appointed by the Board of Directors pursuant to the Capital Markets Legislation for auditing of the accounts and financials of the year 2012;
20. Reading the summary of the Independent Audit Firm's report relating to the fiscal year 2012;
21. Reading, discussion, and approval of the Balance Sheets and Profits/Loss statements relating to the fiscal year 2012;
22. Discussion of and decision on the distribution of dividend for the year 2012 and determination of the dividend distribution date;

23. In accordance with Article 363 of TCC, submittal and approval of the Board Members Elected by the Board of Directors due to vacancies in the Board occurred in the year **2012**;

24. Release of the Board members individually from the activities and operations of the Company pertaining to the year **2012**;

25. Release of the Statutory Auditors individually from activities and operations of the Company pertaining to the year **2012**;

26. Reading the Annual Report of the Board of Directors relating to the fiscal year **2013**;

27. Reading the summary of the Independent Audit Firm's report relating to the fiscal year **2013**;

28. Reading, discussion, and approval of the TCC and CMB Balance Sheets and Profits/Loss statements relating to the fiscal year **2013**;

29. Discussion of and decision on the distribution of dividend for the year **2013** and determination of the dividend distribution date;

30. Release of the Board members individually from the activities and operations of the Company pertaining to the year **2013**;

31. Reading the Annual Report of the Board of Directors relating to the fiscal year 2014;

32. Discussion of and approval of the election of the independent audit firm appointed by the Board of Directors pursuant to TCC and the Capital Markets Legislation for auditing of the accounts and financials of the year 2014;

33. Reading the summary of the Independent Audit Firm's report relating to the fiscal year 2014;

34. Reading, discussion, and approval of the TCC and CMB Balance Sheets and Profits/Loss statements relating to the fiscal year 2014;

35. Discussion of and decision on the distribution of dividend for the year 2014 and determination of the dividend distribution date;

36. Release of the Board members individually from the activities and operations of the Company pertaining to the year 2014;

37. Informing the General Assembly on the donation and contributions made in the years 2011, 2012, 2013, and 2014; approval of donation and contributions made in the years 2013 and 2014; discussion of and decision on the Board of Directors' proposal concerning determination of donation limit to be made in 2015, starting from the fiscal year 2015;

38. Subject to the approval of the Ministry of Customs and Trade and Capital Markets Board; discussion of and decision on the amendment of Articles 3, 4, 6, 7, 8, 9, 10, 11, 12, 13, 14, 15, 16, 17, 18, 19, 21, 24, 25, and 26 of the Articles of Association of the Company;

39. Election of new Board Members in accordance with related legislation and determination of the newly elected Board members' term of office;

40. Determination of the remuneration of the members of the Board of Directors;

41. Discussion of and approval of the election of the independent audit firm appointed by the Board of Directors pursuant to TCC and the Capital Markets Legislation for auditing of the accounts and financials of the year 2015;

*(Continued)*

**Table 2.1** *The agenda of the annual general assembly meeting of Turkcell* **(Continued)**

| |
|---|
| 42. Discussion of and approval of the Internal Guide on General Assembly Rules of Procedures prepared by the Board of Directors; |
| 43. Decision permitting the Board Members to, directly or on behalf of others, be active in areas falling within or outside the scope of the Company's operations and to participate in companies operating in the same business and to perform other acts in compliance with Articles 395 and 396 of the Turkish Commercial Code; |
| 44. Discussion of and approval of the "Dividend Policy of Company" pursuant to the Corporate Governance Principles; |
| 45. Informing the General Assembly on the remuneration rules determined for the Board of Directors and the Senior Management, pursuant to the Corporate Governance Principles; |
| 46. Informing the shareholders regarding the guarantees, pledges, and mortgages provided by the Company to third parties or the derived income thereof, in accordance with the Capital Market Board's regulations; |
| 47. Informing the shareholders on Rule No. 1.3.6 of Corporate Governance Principles; |
| 48. Closing. |

*Source:* http://www.kap.gov.tr/en/search/notice-results.aspx?id=412767, 2015.

# PART II

# External Corporate Governance Mechanisms

# CHAPTER 3

# Formal External Corporate Governance Mechanisms

## Legal Framework on Corporate Governance

Legal system in Turkey is characterized by civil law, underlying the fundamental attributes of the corporate governance system in the country. As a component of the modernization efforts of the Ottoman Empire, the French civil law was adopted in the 19th century.[1] Turkey is among the countries with a civil law origin, a feature associated with a method of social control-based on state desired allocations.[2] Legal origin of the country supports the central role of the state in the Turkish business system.

Corporate governance environment is configured under the combined influence of the legislation including the Turkish Commercial Code (TCC), the Capital Market Law (CML), and the regulations mostly in the form of communiques issued by the Capital Market Board (CMB) of Turkey under the CML. The CML of Turkey, initially enacted in 1981, has recently gone through a revision process, with the new CML coming into force on December 30, 2012. The new CML introduces legislation to strengthen the financial infrastructure in the Turkish capital market and has achieved a significant degree of harmonization with the EU legislation.[3] Additionally, sets of laws for specific industries, such as the banking and telecommunications, also include provisions on corporate governance.[4] The CMB is the leading regulatory authority for setting corporate governance standards for publicly trading companies. It has adopted the Corporate Governance Principles (CGP) in 2003 from the CGP of the Organization for Economic Cooperation and Development (OECD), revised into the current form in 2005. The principles were initially on a "comply-or-explain" basis, but some of the provisions of the CGP became legal requirements as a part of the communique on

Corporate Governance,[5] based on Article 17 of CML, and published in the Official Gazette on January 3, 2014. The communique explicitly states the principles that are compulsory rules for the listed companies. According to the communique, the CMB has the authority to enforce the implementation of the compulsory principles and to take necessary action in the case of transactions that are not in compliance with the compulsory principles. In the case of noncompliance, the CMB is empowered to "ask courts for precautionary legal measures or file a law suit for the execution of the relevant corporate governance rules, or impose administrative pecuniary fines."[6]

The principles not explicitly stated as compulsory remain as guidelines on "comply or explain" basis, where companies are required to explain their reasons for noncompliance and present their amendment plans for the future. The communique also classifies the companies into three categories and provides exemptions to the companies in Group 2 and Group 3 on some of the provisions, keeping the provisions compulsory for companies in Group 1.[7] Classification of companies into three groups are made according to their systematic influence capacity on the market and announced by the CMB, as of January each year, based on calculations made by using their market values and market capitalizations of their shares in free float. Companies with an average market value over 3 billion TL (Turkish lira) and an average market capitalization of shares in the free float over 750 million TL are categorized in Group 1, while the same thresholds for Group 2 companies are 1 billion and 250 million TL, respectively. Group 3 is composed of firms in the Emerging Companies and Watchlist Companies markets in the Borsa Istanbul. These companies are obliged to fulfill the corporate governance compulsory requirements pertaining to their category, and in the case of assignment to a new category, they are expected to meet the corporate governance requirements of their newly assigned categories by the next year following the assignment.[8]

Extensive legislative reforms, including the amendments to the CML in 2011 and 2012 and the communiques on corporate governance based on the new CML, have aimed at improving the corporate governance environment for listed companies. On the other hand, the comprehensive overhaul of the TCC in 2012 has reshaped the corporate governance environment in Turkey for all companies including small and medium-sized enterprises.

The main source of company law in Turkey is the TCC adapted from the Swiss company law in 1957.[9] This code promoted the development of a modern economic order in commercial activity, but it fell behind current advancements in technology and business life, being able to function only through a series of amendments. One of the major drivers behind the modernization of the TCC has been Turkey's EU candidacy, which introduces substantial revisions into the legal system including the TCC.[10] Adoption of a new code has been a lengthy process. Revisions to the TCC were drafted and submitted to the Parliament in 2005 and approved as of January 13, 2011 by the Parliament to be effective on July 1, 2012 with a gradual implementation plan for some of its provisions to be finalized in 2013. Modifications made to the new law before its implementation were enacted on June 30, 2012, one day before the effective date of the new TCC.[11] These modifications canceled or narrowed down some of the provisions of the new TCC. For example, the scope of the compulsory independent audit requirement was narrowed down from all limited liability companies to only large companies, and the requirement for Internet disclosures for nonlisted companies was canceled. Despite the lengthy process in its enactment, the new TCC represents a comprehensive overhaul of the company law in 55 years.

There has been a stubborn resistance to the new TCC from business owners, according to an interview[12] made with one of the prominent law professors, Ünal Tekinalp, who has worked extensively in the preparation of the new law. According to him, business owners have demanded important changes in some of the articles of the new law, such as the requirement on Internet presence for companies, the requirement for publishing auditor report and financial statements on Internet by all companies, and the abolishment of the "shareholders current account" from the accounting system. Transparency requirements of the new law appear to be one of the issues that owners of large companies opposed. In addition, abolishment of the "shareholders current account," an account offering a mechanism to the owner managers to withdraw money from the company, seems to bother some of the businessmen with lobbying power. Tekinalp also observes a presence of a divergence of opinion among the Turkish businessmen with regard to their support of the new law. He states that there is some unrest within family businesses in Anatolia, where some members of the families are in control while other family members are excluded from the management of the companies. Tekinalp claims that these excluded family members strongly support the new TCC, while those in control seem to resist and lobby against it.[13] This opposition and lobbying by businesses have led to the canceling and narrowing down of some of the provisions of the new law before it became effective.

The draft of the new TCC included many provisions on corporate governance, most of which have been enacted and put into effect. Definition of qualifications for becoming a board member, minority rights protection, establishment of proxy voting and electronic voting principles, permission for online general meetings via websites, specification of the minimum informational content required in annual reports and company websites, and the prerequisites regarding the auditors to be independent audit firms or certified public accountants were among the salient corporate governance issues addressed by the draft of TCC.[14] The draft of the new code also introduced the possibility of forming a corporation with a sole shareholder and eventually a board with a sole director. Additionally, the new draft of the TCC contained a comprehensive system for company groups and developed a special liability regime for parent companies.[15]

The new TCC introduces essential legislative changes to board structure and composition.[16] Under the new code, a new corporation type with only one shareholder has become possible. The requirement that the board must have at least three members has consequently been abolished, enabling boards with one member for the newly introduced corporation type with only one shareholder. The code also increases the legal liabilities of the board of directors and introduces sanctions for the board members. The previous TCC and CML did not impose any expertise or education requirements for the directors.[17] The draft of the new TCC had the stipulation that at least one quarter of the members of the board should be university graduates, with the exception of boards with one member. However, this stipulation was abolished in the amendment of the law before it was put into effect.[18] In its existing form, the TCC only requires that board members, including the representatives of corporate members should be competent individuals.[19] On the other hand, the banking law (Law No. 5411, Article 23–25) has expertise and education requirements for bank directors and executives.[20]

The previous TCC and the CML did not have any independence requirements for the board of directors. Consequently, most of the board members in Turkish companies had some kind of relationship with the company either directly or as shareholders.[21] The current TCC does not also include independence requirements for board members. Yet, the new CML empowers the CMB to determine the independence criteria for board members for listed companies. The communique on the CGP issued by the CMB requires the presence of independent members in the board of directors. Accordingly, one-third of the members or at least two directors should be independent members. The new code also eliminates the previous restriction that board members should be shareholders. The communique on Corporate Governance explicitly states the criteria for being designated as an "independent member." The communique also outlines a new mechanism for the approval of independent board members by the CMB in accordance with the independence criteria of the same document. This mechanism is not currently applicable to companies in Groups 2 and 3, out of the three groups defined by the CMB annually based on market value and free float of companies to determine eligibility of companies for different provisions of the CGP.

According to the TCC, all shares have equal voting rights, and the CMB states in the communique on Corporate Governance that "privileges regarding voting rights should be avoided;"[22] and if privileges do exist, they should not be in a manner preventing the shareholders from being represented in the board of directors. The communique requires that the privileges inhibiting the representation of shareholders of publicly traded shares be revoked. Historically speaking, special voting rights or other privileges have been granted to certain classes of shares.[23] Nilsson states that the most frequently used special class privilege seems to be the right to nominate directors to the board.[24] The use of multiple voting rights for founders is one of the mechanisms widely used for maintaining family control.[25] The previous TCC had no restrictions on granting special rights. In a study on the Istanbul Stock Exchange (ISE) companies in 2004, 42 percent of the companies included special class rights to nominate directors in their article of associations.[26] Orbay and Yurtoğlu[27] also report that 43 percent of the companies in their sample have pyramidal ownership structures and dual class shares, thereby departing from the "one share-one vote" rule. The new TCC calls for the use of privileges only for enabling the representation of certain groups of investors or minority shareholders.

Concentrated ownership structure and the presence of dominant family control in the Turkish business context make the expropriation of minority shareholders one of the most important corporate governance issues. However, in the presence of dominant controlling shareholders, many measures on protecting minority shareholders become ineffective.[28] Turkey's performance on minority shareholder protection has been below the average performance of other French origin civil law countries.[29] The current TCC defines shareholders holding a minimum of 10 percent of the shares as minority shareholders for nonlisted companies and 5 percent for listed companies. The previous TCC granted the following rights to the minority shareholders: "the right to ask statutory auditors to investigate allegations, the right to have special auditors appointed, the right to call a shareholder's meeting or to insert items on the agenda, the right to veto the release of director's liabilities due to their transactions during the incorporation of the company and the right to ask the company to sue the directors for their liability." The new code, on the other hand, includes provisions on improving the representation and protection of minority shareholders, but the impacts of the law coming into effect in the second half of 2012 have not yet been documented in literature.

Despite the remarkable improvements in the legislative framework, Turkey's performance in the "rule of law" dimension of the World Governance Indicators is mediocre and deteriorating over time. The normalized scores (between –2.5 and 2.5) of Turkey in the "rule of law" dimension have been 0.13, 0.10, and 0.04 in the years 2004, 2009, and 2014, respectively.[30] These scores correspond to percentile ranks of 57.89, 57.82, and 59.62 out of 100.[31] These figures indicate a deterioration in performance with respect to rule, measuring the extent to which agents have confidence in and abide by the rules of the society, especially in relation to contract enforcement, private property rights, the courts, the police, and the likelihood of crime and violence.[32]

## Regulatory Pressures

Although there have been noteworthy improvements and reforms in the legislative framework and a corresponding growth in the business sector since 2000s, existing regulations in the product and labor markets appear to hinder further development of an open and flexible business environment that would support formal and professional enterprises.[33] "Complex licensing rules for market entry, a limited role for competition policy, restricted competition in network industries and public procurement and rigid employment rules geared to life time employment"[34] are stated as the specific attributes of the existing regulations obstructing the development of a more business-friendly regulatory environment according to the OECD good practices. Gönenç et al.[35] call for improvement in two specific dimensions: making rules for market entry and exit more competition-friendly and improving the transparency and predictability of regulatory enforcement. In accordance with these attributes of the existing system, regulatory quality is mediocre in Turkey, when one takes the World Economic Forum (WEF) International Competitiveness reports, World Bank Doing Business reports, and Governance Indicators into consideration.

According to the Country Economic Profile for Turkey in Global Competitiveness Report of WEF, "inefficient government bureaucracy" and "policy instability" are the first two items in the list of Most Problematic Factors for Doing Business. "Tax regulations" and "restrictive labor regulations" are also mentioned in this list. The Global Competitiveness Index (GCI) of the WEF includes 12 pillars with detailed indicators under each pillar. In 2014–2015, Turkey ranks the 45th out of 144 countries included in the study, with an overall GCI score of 4.46 out of a maximum score of 7[36] and performs similar to or better than other "Emerging and Developing Europe" countries in all the pillars, except for "labor market efficiency." In this dimension, Turkey's score is slightly below the comparable countries. It ranks 131st in "labor market efficiency" dimension, slipping back four ranks since 2010. In this pillar, low level of performance is largely attributable to dimensions of "women in labor force," "redundancy costs," "the country's capacity to attract talent," "effects of taxation on incentives to work," and "cooperation in labor-employer relations."

In the "Doing Business 2015" report of the World Bank,[37] Turkey ranks 55th in 2015 out of 189 counties with respect to its overall performance on the quality of its regulatory framework, four ranks below its 51st rank in 2014. Considering the dimensions of regulatory quality score taking into account all the stages in the life cycle of a business, the country's performance is especially low in areas of "dealing with construction permits," "resolving insolvency," and "getting credits," with ranking of 136th, 109th, and 89th, respectively. On the other hand, Turkey has a relatively good performance on "protecting minority investors," thus ranking 13th on this measure. "Getting electricity" and "enforcing contracts" are the other dimensions of this relatively good performance, where, among 189 countries, Turkey ranks 34th and 38th, respectively.

Comparative evaluations on the regulatory quality in Turkey suggest the necessity for improvements in the existing regulations on product and labor markets for making the environment more supportive for the development of formal and professional businesses. Gönenç et al. assert that tax rules and labor regulations create disincentives for growth and development of businesses.[38] Labor regulations in Turkey are highly rigid and costly, mainly due to the high tax burden on wages. In fact, Turkey has the most strict labor legislation among OECD countries.[39] This feature of the labor market can be a factor encouraging informality. Additionally, the fact that the labor regulation apply unevenly across the spectrum of different types of firms bring about significant economic costs to some businesses as their number of employees exceed certain thresholds. Costly and rigid labor regulations along with informality and uneven application have consequences on the competitive strength of the businesses, thus hindering job creation and economic growth. In order to decrease informality and increase productivity, on the one hand, and to maintaining flexibility in the labor market, on the other, a comprehensive labor market reform agenda was adopted and published as the National Employment Strategy[40] in May 2014 and included this reform package as a strategic priority in the 10th Development Plan for 2014–2018.

In the state-dependent system of Turkey, state monopolies, state-desired allocations in the form of state aids and subsidies as well as public procurement lead to distortions in the competitive environment. Significant regulatory modifications have been made to enhance competition in the market. Turkey has also realized regulatory modifications to enhance competition in markets previously organized as public monopolies, such as the telecommunications and energy industries.[41] There were also significant regulatory modifications in the banking industry following the financial crises of 2000 and 2001, carried out with the aim of creating a sound and stable banking system. The regulations introduced to the banking industry included a series of regulations encompassing four stages, also including a corporate governance related regulation at its last stage.[42] Turkey has also introduced regulations in the areas of state aid subsidies and public procurement legislation. Yet, implementation of these has remained limited and thus contradicted with the EU acquis in the case of the recent amendments to the public procurement legislation.[43]

## External Auditing

Related party transactions are a critical governance issue in the Turkish business context dominated by family-controlled groups of companies. Considering the fact that related party transactions are defined in a principles-based manner in the International Financial Reporting Standards, the judgments of independent auditors become vital for effective corporate governance. However, identifying related party transactions and resulting expropriation by controlling owners remains as a difficult task for the auditors, which thus increases the need for a sound regulatory framework and improved audit standards.

The new TCC introduced a group of provisions on accounting and auditing. Previously, only publicly listed companies were required to go through compulsory audits by independent audit firms. Other joint stock companies and limited partnerships were subject to internal audit, which was performed by controllers without any specifications for controllers.[44] The new TCC, however, extended the compulsory independent audit requirement to all capital stock companies, including the nonlisted companies and the state-owned enterprises.[45]

Institutional structure for regulating accounting and auditing has also improved.[46] Accounting and auditing standards were previously regulated by various agencies, including the Turkish Accounting Standards Board and the Turkish Audit Standards Board. Having abolished these agencies, a new regulatory and supervisory agency titled the "Public Oversight, Accounting and Auditing Standards Authority" was established in November 2011. This new institution has the authority to issue accounting and auditing standards, to certify independent auditors and audit firms, and to perform public oversight of independent audits.[47] National auditing standards in accordance with the International Standards on Auditing (ISA) have been drafted by this newly established regulatory authority.[48] Independent auditors of publicly listed companies are also subject to additional criteria and supervision by the CMB.

## Market for Corporate Control

The market for corporate control is inactive. In the business context of Turkey characterized by a weak protection of minority shareholders, business owners hold concentrated ownership structures. Takeover risks are therefore low in the market. In most cases, it is not possible to take over a company without the consent of the controlling shareholders. Thus, the market does not act as a disciplining mechanism in the case of poor performance.[49]

Institutional investors can be expected to perform monitoring and to have disciplinary effects on companies through various mechanisms they might utilize. However, investor base is limited and domestic institutional investments are scarce, despite the recent efforts of the government to promote private savings and increase domestic institutional investments through a private pension incentive scheme in 2012.[50] Given the limited domestic investor base, another group that might have monitoring impact on companies is the foreign institutional investors, which have considerable stakes in the listed companies in the ISE. Empirical findings on better voluntary disclosure in companies with higher foreign institutional investment might suggest for a monitoring role of the foreign institutional investors.[51]

# CHAPTER 4

# Informal External Corporate Governance Mechanisms

Corporate governance practices are also influenced by informal external institutions of the Turkish context. Sociocultural norms, news media, and corporate governance codes may all act as some of the important factors informally shaping governance activities of different organizations.

## Sociocultural Norms

Patriarchy and paternalism are prominent characteristics of Turkish society and Turkish business system. The father presents a central figure in family as well as in the patriarchal organization of the family firms in Turkey. He is able to offer or to impede access to resources and to shape career choices of the children. This can be easily observed in family firms where the father decides on the career path of the family members. Typically, the father's assertiveness is not even questioned. Children are not expected to resist their fathers' decisions, with the cultural assumption that the fathers' decisions are for their good. This is also in line with the assertive nature of the Turkish society. High levels of dominance and toughness have been increasingly characterizing the Turkish society since the last 40 years, despite the fact that the "people in society aspire for tender and nonassertive relationships."[1]

One must also point out to the paternalistic features of Turkish management culture.[2] Turkey has been observed to be highly paternalistic along with Pakistan, China, and India.[3] Paternalism determines the relationship between the superior and the subordinate. Superiors are expected to make decisions for the subordinate's welfare, and subordinates in turn are expected to obey and show commitment to their superiors.[4] Superiors are also found to believe that the subordinates are by nature prone to make progress if they are given the necessary opportunities, to assume responsibility and participate in the decision-making process.[5] The former have personalized relationships with the subordinates, thus being able to discuss with the latter both family and work issues, an exchange enabling subordinates to be consulted. However, the implementation of their suggestions is not as frequent.[6] Superiors are seen as older members of the family limiting subordinates' proactive actions. The latter only act reactively and do not take initiatives given that there is an authority figure to take the right decisions for them.[7] Both patriarchy and paternalism may have a significant impact on corporate governance practices by limiting the participation of different stakeholder groups (such as employees, minority shareholders) in the decision-making process. They may also act as mechanisms impeding reaction in cases of governance misconducts performed by the superiors.

Several studies depicted high power distance, low individualism, and high uncertainty avoidance as the main characteristics of Turkish context.[8] In communities scoring high in power distance unequal distribution of power and influence are tolerated. For instance, the differences in status or wage are perceived as normal. Similarly, the incidence of hierarchical systems such as stock pyramids in Turkish corporate governance is associated with high power distance score.[9] Leadership is typically exercised through hierarchy, authority is very much respected, and high power distance between managers and their subordinates leaves no room for equal standing in both remuneration and decision making in Turkey.[10] Subordinates do not feel comfortable in expressing themselves to their superiors and avoid voicing their disagreement. Both Turkish companies and the Turkish society are hierarchical.[11] Assertiveness is another characteristic supporting hierarchical structures. Furthermore, top managers do not seem to delegate power, according to the Global Competitiveness Report of World Economic Forum. On a 7-point scale where 1 indicates that "senior management takes all important decisions" and 7 indicates that "authority is mostly delegated to business unit heads and other lower level managers," Turkey scored 3.6 and ranked 56 among 144 countries.[12]

In societies with a high score on uncertainty avoidance index, conflict and competition tend to be avoided. It is associated, for example, with the opaque disclosure in governance[13] through which conflict and competition are avoided. According to the GLOBE study, performance orientation is low, meaning that the Turkish society does not motivate people to constantly make progress and does little "to reward performance effectiveness and achievement."[14] The same study reports a low future orientation score, delineating the tendency to accept life incidents as they happen rather than to plan for the future. This tendency can be partly explained by the Islamic rule of believing in fate commanding to accept life as it unfolds.[15] Interesting to note is that the results of the GLOBE study also show an aspiration for planning, as managers believe they should plan. However, the high uncertainty level prevailing in the country due to unplanned activities of the state, frequent policy changes, economic and political turmoil, all make planning objectives and intentions hard to achieve.

Values of the Turkish society present both continuity and change since the 1990s. Yılmaz Esmer's study displays the values of the Turkish society and their relative change.[16] His study provides evidence on trust level, religion, gender equality, and conservatism that can be summarized as follows.

Turkey is among the countries scoring the lowest in interpersonal trust. Only one in 10 people reports to trust others. This ratio varies from one region to other, being highest in Central Anatolia (16 percent), and lowest in the Aegean region and Thrace (7 percent). Furthermore, Turkish society is found to be amongst the most religious countries in Europe. However, 64 percent think that religion is about obedience to the rules rather than doing "good," and it is perceived as ascribing meaning to afterlife by 76 percent. Conservatism, which was assessed along the dimensions such as religion, family, women's rights, sexual freedom, nationalism, authoritarian tendency, political ideology, and fatalism/freewill, seems to have increased from 60.34 in 1996 to 63.00 in 2011 over a scale of 100. Interesting to note is that conservatism appears to have increased mostly among the university graduates (from 38.5 in 1996 to 54.8 in 2011). Slight improvements are observed in tolerance (3.38 to 4.02) and in the social status of women (2.62 to 3.01) from 1996 to 2011.

Turkey ranks 48th out of 60 countries in terms of gender equality. Those who claim that man should be the leader of the family constitute

81 and 71 percent, respectively, among men and women. About 69 percent of men and 59 percent of women believe that women should always obey their husbands. However, 65 percent of men and 69 percent of women reject the idea that university education is more important for their sons. The ratio of those who believe that priority should be given to men in case of unemployment has fallen to 60 percent in 2011 from 67 percent in 1996. According to the Global Gender Gap Report, Turkey has the 125th position among 142 countries in relation to economic opportunity and participation presented to women. Thus, female participation in labor force is still low, with a lingering glass ceiling for top management positions.

In their study, Aycan et al.[17] also claim that the cultural traits of the Turkish population have been undergoing a change and they are now moderately collectivistic and hierarchical. The Turkish urban population shows signs of a move toward individualism, achievement, and increased competition.[18] Similarly, Turkish students rated entrepreneurship values higher than American students, a shift that is usually perceived to have been led by the drastic policy change toward liberalism in Turkey after 1980.[19] They also scored high in Protestant work ethic, which is consistent with Aslan's[20] comparative findings for Turkish Muslim managers found to place more importance on hard work, time, and money saving, and to adopt a negative attitude toward leisure compared with their British and Irish counterparts.

Furthermore, according to a recent study, the managers consider integrity, valuing competency, and achievement as the most proper values, and cliquishness, laziness, and favoritism as the most improper ones.[21] As the organizational size gets smaller, the internalization and practicing of these values tend to increase.

The sociocultural traits of the Turkish society have important repercussions on corporate governance. Through its moderately collectivistic and hierarchical structure, together with its paternalism and patriarchy, the Turkish context creates relatively submissive employees and ineffective boards in the companies who do not dare challenging authority and reacting to unfavorable governance practices. One other informal external control mechanism to chase misbehaviors in governance is news media, which is also firmly embedded within this sociocultural context.

# News Media

Since the beginning of the press in the late Ottoman era, government restrictions on freedom of expression and freedom of press have been frequent in Turkey.[22] Upto 1980, newspapers owned by families such as Simavi, Karacan, and Nadi (whose origins dated back to the late Ottoman era when their founders, as young intellectual/journalists, had started a career in publishing) dominated the media sector.[23] These families acquired substantial cultural and social capitals with their intellectual prestige and political influence, but they could not accumulate economic wealth[24] as would their post-1980 counterparts in media sector. Low newspaper sales and economic weaknesses made them vulnerable to the pressure of the government, which could control them through printing paper subsidies, credits from state financial institutions, and selective allocation of official publicity.[25] The Turkish Press' long and intricate relations with the state, army, political elite, and dominant economic actors increased in scope and scale after 1980 (i.e., with the transition to liberal economic policy) when businessmen started to buy media outlets and the notion of "elite executive journalists" was introduced.[26]

During the years between 1990 and 1994, media sector went through a period of rapid deregulation and conglomeration.[27] Following the deregulation, media owners started to put pressure on politicians through their media outlets, which meant the inversion of the so-far established relationship between state and media.[28] The involvement of corporations in the media sector was rather linked with the indirect and lucrative benefits of ownership than with a desire to create a democratic media.[29] However, these same concentrated ownership and conglomeration characteristics generated, after a while, an obedient press in the face of government demands. Media owners and "elite executive journalists" applied pressures on editorial decision making and promoted self-censorship[30] with an eye to protect their own business interests.

Actually, there is a strong government pressure on media. Turkey ranks 149 (out of 180 countries) according to the World Press Freedom Index, and it is among the countries with the highest number of its journalists in prison.[31] Even the most renowned journalists are dismissed because of their criticisms regarding government policies. The organization of

Reporters Without Borders identifies major drawbacks in Turkey as the repressive legal practices against the members of the press, lack of democratic culture among the security forces, growing concentration of media ownership by the businessmen linked to the government.[32]

The ownership structure of the media sector appears to be the main factor behind the tight control of the government. The sector is distinguished by the domination of large media holdings with significant nonmedia investments. Cross ownership is not restrained in Turkey. The media owners prefer fulfilling the requests of the government to avoid penalties such as substantial tax fines. For example, the Doğan Group, one of the dominant media conglomerates in Turkey, has pursued its critics in spite of the threats of the former prime minister (President of the Republic since 2015) and ended up with being accused of tax evasion and received a tax fine of more than two billion dollars.[33] This may give a single but striking idea about the potential costs of challenging the government.

On the other hand, there are also incentives for those adopting a self-censorship policy. Every holding company investing in the media sector profits from government contracts, like in the following examples:[34] Doğuş Holding (NTV, StarTV) obtained a $702 million bid in May 2013 to operate the Galataport in the center of Istanbul. İhlas Holding (possessing *Türkiye*, the İhlas News Agency, and the TGRT TV) obtained a government contract of $1.86 billion deal to redevelop a district in Istanbul. These media holdings dependent on government contracts and regulations are thus open to government pressure to lower their criticism and dismiss critical journalists. Furthermore, another important incentive is the revenues obtained from state-owned companies' advertising. The Nielsen AdEx reports point out that government-friendly media groups enjoy a considerably higher percentage of state-owned enterprises' advertising budget.

Moreover, after the banking crisis in 2001, many media outlets were taken over by the state and they thus became the subject to an indirect government control. The government distributed "some of these media outlets to loyal businessmen who had won several government tenders during the AKP administrations and had significantly expanded their businesses."[35] The government intervention is very strong in such media outlets. For example, the headlines are even dictated by the government, which can result in several newspapers to have the same headlines on some days.

As the factors contributing to poor development of freedom of press in Turkey, Çatalbaş identifies:

> ideological and socio-cultural background of journalists; the issues of democratic governance, representation and de-unionization within news organizations; ineffectiveness of journalists associations; organizational and internalized self-censorship mechanisms; near non-existence of local press, and the prevailing excessively commercial media culture, which perceives and presents news as part of the show business.[36]

Christensen[37] also identifies the major problems of freedom of speech as the ownership concentration in the media sector, owners' efforts to de-unionize journalists and government legislation restraining the rights of news workers.

Similarly, Öncü[38] summarizes the characteristics of the current media as:

1. A very narrowly based but politically active press.
2. Overwhelming dominance of commercial/tabloid television.
3. Media conglomerates with links to diverse sectors of the economy.
4. Political polarization in the public domain with continuing struggles over media ownership and regulation.

Given the amount of restrictions in the main stream news media, many journalists who were dismissed or forced out due to their critical coverage of the government and its policies started to write on Internet news media. However, Internet penetration is about 51 percent for the 77.2 million inhabitants of the country, a figure that is not quite high.[39] Especially during the last years, there have been severe limitations on accessing and developing Internet news media. In September 2014, the Law No. 5651 on Regulating the Internet was modified to provide authorities with the possibility of accessing user data without a warrant. This modification was soon overturned by the Constitutional Court.

However, as the court's chief judge retired in March 2015, it was passed again. This allowed authorities to ban content without necessitating a court order for reasons of national security, public health safety, and crime prevention.[40] The Freedom House provides some interesting information about the Internet freedom score in Turkey, regressing to 58 (1: best and 100: worst) in 2015 from 49 in 2013.[41] Social media, and political/social content are frequently blocked. Turkey has been for a period among the countries banning Twitter and YouTube. During the first six months of 2015, 92 percent of court orders about content removal received by Twitter came from Turkey.[42] Bloggers and ICT (information and communication technologies) users get arrested for their comments in social media. Particularly after the Gezi protests in 2013, the relation between the government and the media became increasingly strained, with the former adopting repressive actions such as open threats to alleged opponents, silencing major media outlets by financial threats, censorship,[43] physical aggression to media members, and investigations on terrorism charges.[44] Given all these restrictions, press freedom is categorized as "not free" by the Freedom House.[45]

Briefly stated, press freedom in Turkey seems to be under escalating threat.[46] This partly originates from the restricting laws and regulations, but the weakness is also due to the inherent structure of the media sector making it open to influences and pressures of capital owners and politicians.[47] As a matter of fact, the government's conception of capitalism is determined on the basis of a strong shareholder capitalism, privileging the shareholders and especially the capitalists loyal to the government at the detriment of other stakeholders such as employees, customers, community, and so on. Frequent violations of worker/employee rights and serious corporate governance scandals such as handing over a government company to loyal businessmen by using state funds receive limited coverage in mainstream news media. As can be understood from all we have mentioned thus far, the combination of state and corporate influence has a well-documented role in the suppression of freedom of expression and freedom of press in Turkey. Through its ever-restrictive laws, the state makes it impossible "for investigative journalists to, for example, expose political or military corruption, or to implicate a public official in criminal activity, without running the risk of themselves being convicted of a crime."[48] Although there are still some critical media outlets such as *Cumhuriyet*, *Sözcü*, and *Birgün* (each with a different ideology or affiliation), they are often chastised and their journalists are investigated for charges in relation to terrorism or illegal actions against the government. Some are imprisoned, some receive life threats, and some are even physically attacked. Thus, the oppression ranges from assaults to media headquarters by the supporters of the ruling party,[49] physical attacks to the journalists, incarceration with charges of terrorism and/or espionage,[50] limiting the broadcasting opportunities of dissident TV channels by canceling their access to satellites and takeover of pro-opposition media outlets by the government.

In spite of the limitations to free press, the Turkish media sector is estimated to be worth of a market of 11.6 billion with a growth potential of 11.4 percent per year, which is the double of the global average.[51] Yet, daily sale is around 96 newspapers per a population of 1,000 people, ranking the lowest in Europe.[52] Around 81 percent of the newspaper circulation is made by the national newspapers based in two major cities Istanbul and Ankara, and about a dozen of them lead the discussions on domestic politics and international matters.[53]

These figures imply a potential in news media, which can really have a critical role in chasing incidences of violation of stakeholder rights in all types of organizations, something that is actually done to a very limited degree due to the aforementioned restrictions. The sad truth is that these forms of oppressions limit the role of news media in detecting governance problems.

## Corporate Governance Codes

Corporate governance is mainly regulated by the Turkish Commercial Code together with the Turkish Capital Markets Law and the Capital Market Board (CMB) Communiqués. Since the current legal framework fails to fully address governance issues, the Corporate Governance Principles (CGP) have become the basis of the corporate governance practices in Turkey.

In 2000, the Turkish Businessmen and Industrialists Association (TÜSİAD) was the first to publish a report on the Organization for Economic Cooperation and Development (OECD) CGP.[54] However, external pressures seem to have been more influential on the initiatives for adopting governance principles in Turkey. In 2001, one of the conditions of the stabilization package, relating to the stand-by credit from the International Monetary Fund (IMF), compelled Turkey to launch "good governance" in both private and public sectors.[55] In the early 2000s, Turkey was the only OECD country without a governance code.[56] This diffusionist pressure seems to have impacted Turkish regulatory authorities. In 2003, the CMB published the CGP based on the OECD CGP and revised them in 2005. Publicly held enterprises were required to report their compliance with the CMB Principles together with their annual report starting from 2004, and this became a regular requisite from 2009 onward.[57] The CMB indicates that improving the corporate governance environment and integrating Turkish capital markets with global markets are the main objectives in the preparation of the governance principles. Hence, attracting foreign investment and having access to international funds appear as the main motivators.[58] It may therefore be concluded that the adoption of governance principles was more for the sake of external actors than internal constituents. It is also worth mentioning that the CGP is based on the internationally accepted good governance principles, and that it does not address the most relevant governance issues in Turkey. A comparison[59] with the German principles would reveal that Turkish principles focus more on the role of the international investors and capital markets. While the Turkish CGP refers to the equal treatment of stakeholders, the focus is still on the shareholder rights. This seems to be consistent with the initial aim of introducing CGP in Turkey, which focused on attracting foreign capital and accessing international funds.

As is the case in many other countries, Turkish governance principles apply only to listed companies. The CMB stepped recently from the "comply or explain" approach to the mandatory approach.[60] Listed companies (except for the Watch List and Emerging Companies market) are categorized under three groups depending on their free float and market value. The provisions are mandatory for the first category and applicable with certain exemptions for the second and third categories. Compliance report (Kurumsal Uyum Raporu) is an important part of the annual report, which is mandatory disclosure.

Therefore, the Capital Market Law and/or the communiqués of the CMB and the new Commercial Code made some of the CGPs mandatory. Thus, the CGP represents a blend of voluntary and mandatory provisions, which according to an OECD report,[61] is among the factors limiting the effectiveness of CGP.

The CMB presents the CGP under four headings (shareholders, public disclosure and transparency, stakeholders, and board of directors) and provides the framework for corporate governance practices. As the corporate governance process is relatively recent phenomenon, many companies experience difficulties in understanding and implementing them. For example, Arçelik, one of the largest manufacturing companies with a score of 9.4/10 in compliance index, states in its compliance report that they experience difficulties in applying some provisions due to practical difficulties, debates about some principles at the local and international level, and the incompatibility of the principles with the company structure and the Turkish market.[62] Turkish management culture is also cited as an impeding factor to adopt CGPs.[63] Companies tend to implement the easy-to-do changes, and the principles relating to important conflicts of interests are often neglected.[64] The level of voluntary disclosure appears to be very low.[65] While profitability positively influences voluntary disclosure, size affects it in a negative way in listed companies.[66] To improve transparency, the Public Disclosure Platform (KAP—Kamuyu Aydın-latma Platformu) was launched as a project of the Capital Market Board, Istanbul Stock Exchange (now Borsa İstanbul), the Turkish Information Technologies and Electronics Research Institute (BILTEN), and started its test runs in 2004.[67] After a transition period, starting from the first day of 2010, companies have been required to send all disclosure only to the KAP.[68] Through the use of digital certificates and electronic signatures, all disclosures of listed companies are disseminated electronically on this electronic system.

To promote the implementation of CGP, the Istanbul Stock Exchange (ISE; now Borsa İstanbul) launched in 2007 a Corporate Governance Index (CGI) including listed companies, which obtained a score of at least 7 out of 10.[69] The index measures price and return performance of the companies obtaining an overall 7 over 10 or at least 6.5 over 10 on each main heading. Companies fulfilling the requirements to become included in the CGI in accordance with the evaluation of the authorized grading institutions receive a quotation fee discount, which is 50 percent for the first two years, 25 percent for the following two years, and finally 10 percent subsequently. As of January 2015, the CGI comprised 49 companies whose names, activity domains, rating agencies, and rating scores are presented in Table 4.1. Rating firms authorized by the CMB evaluate the companies. SAHA seems to be most frequently preferred rating institution. Others are JSR EURASIA rating, KOBIRATE, TÜRK KREDİ rating, and Institutional Shareholder Services (ISS). Sectoral breakdown of companies included in the CGI indicates the presence of both financial and manufacturing companies, together with a number of companies from retailing, technology, transportation, communication, and construction industries.

It is also worth noting that corporate governance ratings are not systematically used by the investors,[70] and that no performance difference is observed between the CGI companies and their counterparts in ISE 50. This may partly explain the companies' limited interest in the CGI.

Nevertheless, the CGI companies also perceive advantages in taking part in the index. For example, top executives and directors of the Doğan Media Corporation report that CGI membership increased the value and the legitimacy of their company, which in turn resulted in an increased interest from foreign investors and international funds.[71] They also claim that through their enhanced communication with foreign counterparts, they were able to improve their business model and also to have access to less expensive credit sources.

Generally speaking, Turkish corporations do not seem to be enthusiastic in embracing the CGP. A careful investigation of compliance reports demonstrate that they try to provide minimum amount of information to fulfill the requirements. This lack of enthusiasm is also due to the sociocultural characteristics such as uncertainty avoidance, high power distance, and collectivism, which are all expected to result in a preference for hierarchical systems, weak disclosure practices, undeveloped mechanisms to

Table 4.1 Corporate governance index companies in January 2015

| Name of Company | Industry | First Rating | | | Last Rating | | |
|---|---|---|---|---|---|---|---|
| | | Date | Rating | Rating Institution | Date | Rating | Rating Institution |
| Vestel Elektronik | Manufacturing | 01.03.2007 | 75,91 | ISIS | 23.02.2015 | 91,24 | SAHA |
| Yeşil GMYO | Financial | 20.04.2007 | 78,83 | SAHA | 17.04.2015 | 91,77 | SAHA |
| Tofaş Türk | Manufacturing | 28.05.2007 | 70,72 | SAHA | 05.11.2014 | 90,09 | SAHA |
| Türk Traktör | Manufacturing | 23.08.2007 | 75,17 | SAHA | 15.08.2014 | 90,46 | SAHA |
| HÜRRİYET GAZETESİ | Manufacturing | 01.09.2007 | 79,67 | ISS | 24.09.2014 | 92,96 | SAHA |
| TÜPRAŞ | Manufacturing | 08.10.2007 | 79,12 | SAHA | 02.10.2014 | 93,10 | SAHA |
| OTOKAR | Manufacturing | 20.03.2008 | 79,40 | SAHA | 19.03.2015 | 92,81 | SAHA |
| ANADOLU EFES | Manufacturing | 11.06.2008 | 80,96 | SAHA | 22.05.2015 | 95,49 | SAHA |
| YAPI VE KREDİ BANKASI | Financial | 29.12.2008 | 80,21 | SAHA | 29.12.2014 | 92,51 | SAHA |
| ŞEKERBANK | Financial | 27.02.2009 | 81,36 | ISS | 06.02.2015 | 91,10 | KOBİRATE |
| COCA COLA İÇECEK | Manufacturing | 01.07.2009 | 83,04 | SAHA | 01.07.2015 | 94,02 | SAHA |
| ARÇELİK | Manufacturing | 30.07.2009 | 82,09 | SAHA | 23.07.2014 | 94,11 | SAHA |
| TAV HAVA LİMANLARI | Financial | 04.09.2009 | 83,34 | ISS | 21.08.2015 | 95,19 | SAHA |
| T.S.K.B | Financial | 20.10.2009 | 87,69 | SAHA | 20.10.2014 | 94,43 | SAHA |
| DOĞAN HOLDİNG | Financial | 03.11.2009 | 82,64 | SAHA | 05.11.2014 | 93,53 | SAHA |
| PETKİM | Manufacturing | 05.11.2009 | 77,13 | TÜRK KREDİ | 19.08.2015 | 90,30 | KOBİRATE |
| LOGO YAZILIM | Technology | 22.12.2009 | 80,53 | SAHA | 15.12.2014 | 90,29 | SAHA |
| İŞ FİN. KİR. | Financial | 28.12.2009 | 80,24 | SAHA | 26.12.2014 | 90,68 | SAHA |
| TURK TELEKOM | Communication | 28.12.2009 | 80,11 | SAHA | 12.12.2014 | 87,24 | SAHA |
| PRYSMIAN KABLO | Manufacturing | 29.12.2009 | 77,58 | SAHA | 05.12.2014 | 90,62 | SAHA |
| TURCAS PETROL | Manufacturing | 12.03.2010 | 75,20 | KOBİRATE | 03.03.2015 | 92,70 | KOBİRATE |
| PARK ELEK. MADENCİLİK | Mining | 09.06.2010 | 86,45 | SAHA | 05.06.2015 | 90,29 | SAHA |
| AYGAZ | Manufacturing | 30.06.2010 | 84,61 | SAHA | 01.07.2015 | 93,58 | SAHA |

(Continued)

*Table 4.1 Corporate governance index companies in January 2015   (Continued)*

| Company | Sector | Date | Rating | Agency | Date | Rating | Agency |
|---|---|---|---|---|---|---|---|
| ALBARAKA TÜRK | Financial | 21.10.2010 | 81,38 | JCR EURASIA | 04.03.2014 | 83,39 | JCR EURASIA |
| YAZICILAR HOLDING | Financial | 08.11.2010 | 80,44 | SAHA | 09.10.2014 | 91,30 | SAHA |
| İHLAS EV ALETLERİ | Manufacturing | 28.12.2010 | 71,20 | JCR EURASIA | 03.03.2014 | 77,96 | JCR EURASIA |
| İHLAS HOLDING | Financial | 28.12.2010 | 77,10 | JCR EURASIA | 03.03.2014 | 78,73 | JCR EURASIA |
| DOĞUŞ OTOMOTİV | Retailing | 01.02.2011 | 77,05 | TÜRK KREDİ | 15.12.2014 | 92,50 | KOBİRATE |
| PINAR SÜT | Manufacturing | 24.11.2011 | 83,43 | SAHA | 20.11.2014 | 90,93 | SAHA |
| EGELİ& CO. YATIRIM HOLDİNG | Financial | 02.12.2011 | 82,00 | SAHA | 28.11.2014 | 92,44 | SAHA |
| T. HALK BANKASI | Financial | 19.12.2011 | 87,40 | SAHA | 19.12.2014 | 91,93 | SAHA |
| İŞ Y. MEN. DEĞ. | Financial | 23.12.2011 | 86,29 | JCR EURASIA | 05.09.2014 | 89,09 | JCR EURASIA |
| GLOBAL YATIRIM HOLDING | Financial | 28.12.2011 | 83,64 | SAHA | 26.11.2014 | 88,80 | KOBİRATE |
| GARANTİ FAKTORİNG | Financial | 23.08.2012 | 83,58 | KOBİRATE | 20.08.2015 | 91,50 | KOBİRATE |
| ENKA İNŞAAT | Construction | 26.11.2012 | 91,59 | SAHA | 20.11.2014 | 90,22 | SAHA |
| PINAR ET VE UN | Manufacturing | 07.12.2012 | 87,73 | SAHA | 21.11.2014 | 91,13 | SAHA |
| BOYNER MAĞAZACILIK | Retailing | 10.12.2012 | 86,36 | SAHA | 10.12.2014 | 89,51 | SAHA |
| ASELSAN | Technology | 13.12.2012 | 87,73 | SAHA | 12.12.2014 | 90,94 | SAHA |
| İŞ GMYO | Financial | 27.12.2012 | 85,27 | JCR EURASIA | 04.12.2014 | 90,92 | SAHA |
| GARANTİ YAT. ORT. | Financial | 21.01.2013 | 83,90 | KOBİRATE | 26.12.2014 | 92,10 | KOBİRATE |
| CREDIWEST FAKTORING | Financial | 24.06.2013 | 80,28 | JCR EURASIA | 12.06.2015 | 82,17 | JCR EURASIA |
| PINAR SU | Manufacturing | 04.12.2013 | 93,41 | SAHA | 05.12.2014 | 92,77 | SAHA |
| PEGASUS | Transportation | 31.12.2013 | 81,30 | KOBİRATE | 24.10.2014 | 87,70 | KOBİRATE |
| ÇEMAŞ DÖKÜM | Manufacturing | 28.05.2014 | 76,20 | KOBİRATE | 27.05.2015 | 80,00 | KOBİRATE |
| AKSA | Manufacturing | 05.08.2014 | | SAHA | 23.07.2015 | 95,00 | SAHA |
| A KİŞ GMYO | Financial | 21.11.2014 | 91,57 | SAHA | 21.11.2014 | 91,57 | SAHA |
| GARANTİ BANKASI | Financial | 11.12.2014 | 91,41 | JCR EURASIA | 11.12.2014 | 91,41 | JCR EURASIA |
| ŞİŞE CAM | Financial | 29.12.2014 | 92,78 | SAHA | 29.12.2014 | 92,78 | SAHA |
| İZOCAM | Manufacturing | 30.12.2014 | 87,60 | KOBİRATE | 30.12.2014 | 87,60 | KOBİRATE |

*Source:* Borsa İstanbul, 2015.[72]

impede self-dealing, and finally boards typified by principal–steward relationship.[73] In line with these assertions, what is observed in the Turkish business system is not voluntarism but a top-down policy whereby business owners believe that good governance practices can only be adopted after the fine-tuning of "legal, cultural, and institutional infrastructure."[74]

# PART III

# Internal Corporate Governance Mechanisms

# CHAPTER 5

# Ownership in the Turkish Economy

## Typical Ownership Concentration

The Turkish business context is characterized by a lower protection of property rights, weaker regulatory environments with ineffective enforcement of regulations[1,2] and lower levels of economic and political stability, which are all typical to emerging market settings. All these attributes are associated with a strategy of social control in economy through state-desired allocations rather than private market-based outcomes,[3] and a context with a limited capital base, high cost of capital, difficult access to finance, and weak financial infrastructure. Accordingly, the business landscape in Turkey is largely dominated by small and medium-sized enterprises (SMEs) with a low share of large companies. A report by the European Commission[4] identifies 3,506 large companies in 2011, which correspond to 0.1 percent of the total number of companies and account for 24.3 percent of the total number of employees and 47.1 percent of total value added. The overwhelming majority of these large companies is privately held.

Similar to other emerging markets, where large block holders dominate the ownership structure of firms,[5,6] companies in Turkey have highly concentrated ownership structures.[7,8,9] Owners hold a high percentage of shares, as maintaining control over the company through internal mechanisms becomes critical in a context with a weaker protection of private property rights and ineffective enforcement of regulations. In the state-dependent business system of Turkey,[10] controlling owners are generally families. In fact, in Istanbul Stock Exchange (ISE), more than 75 percent of companies are owned by families retaining the majority control.[11]

Besides holding the majority of cash flow rights, family owned companies utilize three major ways to retain control: issuing privileged shares, organizing a pyramidal ownership structure, and cross-shareholdings.[12] These mechanisms create a potential for the expropriation of minority shareholders by the controlling families. Hence, in such a highly concentrated and family dominated ownership structure, the major agency issue is between the controlling shareholders and minority shareholders, rather than the managers and shareholders.

Listed companies in Turkey generally maintain control over their companies through holding the majority of both voting rights and cash flow rights. Thus, the wedge between cash flow rights and voting rights is relatively low[13,14] and cash flow rights and voting rights are more aligned as compared to other family controlled business systems such as those in Italy and various East Asian countries.[15] In the 100 largest companies of the ISE in 1999, the average voting rights were 66 percent, while the average cash flow rights were 52 percent in the 68 family-controlled companies as documented by Demirağ and Sertel.[16] According to this result, the average control leverage ratio that they calculate by dividing control rights to cash flow rights is 1.26, which is similar to the "wedge," calculated as the difference between control and cash flow rights for civil law origin countries in the study by La Porta, Lopez-de-Silanes, Shleifer, and Vishny.[17]

Concentration of ownership seems to increase over time. Ownership structure of listed companies became more concentrated from 1999 to 2009.[18] There has been a considerable increase in the cash flow rights controlled by the single largest shareholder. The average share of the largest owner, which was 43.8 percent in 1999, increased to 46.2 percent in 2009 considering all the companies listed in the ISE as of the given year. Together with the rise in the share of the largest owner, the share of the dispersed owners, namely the shares of free float, also increased during the period, indicating a decline in the share of other significant block holders than the largest shareholder. The average share of free float increased from 33.7 percent in 1999 to 39.1 percent in 2009.

The average share of dispersed owners in listed companies stayed around this level following the period covered in the research, displaying a slight increase in recent years, reaching 39.3 percent as of the end of

2014, according to a report[19] by the Turkish Investor Relations Society (TÜYİD) and Central Securities Depository Institution (MKK). While the BIST-30, BIST-50, and BIST-100 index companies conform to the average dispersed owner shares in the total sample, there are sectoral differences in the average of free float. The lowest average share of dispersed owners is observed for technology and service sector companies, with 24.1 and 34.6 percent shares in free float, respectively. The highest average of dispersed owners of 50.7 percent is observed for trading companies. The share of the dispersed owners stayed about the same level of around 39 percent over the period between 2009 and 2014, leaving a significant control share for the block holders in the ownership structure of listed companies. Moreover, it is not possible to claim that companies with a large share of free float in their ownership structure are without a controlling owner. Even in such cases, a company affiliated with a business group or a coalition of shareholders is able to maintain control over the company through various mechanisms such as special voting rights.

While the shares of the largest owner and that of free float increased since 1999, the average share of the block holders except for the largest shareholder decreased from 22.5 to 14.6 percent between 1999 and 2009. Rising ownership concentration is also apparent in the increase in the number of companies controlled with more than 50 percent of the shares. There were 116 companies in 1999 in the ISE, which were controlled with more than 50 percent of cash flow rights. In 2009, the number of companies with majority control increased, reaching up to 139. Indicators on ownership concentration for listed companies in 1999 and 2009 are displayed in Table 5.1.

*Table 5.1 Ownership concentration of Turkish listed companies*

| | Controlled with more than 50% of shares | Largest shareholder | Other shareholders (shareholders other than largest owner and market) | Market (dispersed shares) |
|---|---|---|---|---|
| | # of firms | % | % | % |
| 1999 | 116 | 43.76 | 22.53 | 33.71 |
| 2009 | 139 | 46.22 | 14.64 | 39.14 |

Source: Yamak and Ertuna (2012).[20]

Another indication of the increased concentration relates to the changes in the ownership structure of business groups. As the dominant form of ownership in the ISE, the average shareholdings of business groups increased from 53 percent in 1999 to 54.6 percent in 2009,[21] indicating a stronger control of business groups by their majority shareholders.

## Typical Dominant Owners

Typical dominant owners are families. However, state ownership is also an important aspect of the large businesses in Turkey. In her list of the 50 largest economic players, Colpan[22] identifies two pillars in the large enterprise economy in Turkey, including diversified business groups and state-owned enterprises. Turkey is categorized as a state-dependent business system according to the typology of Whitley,[23] and displays the basic features of this system. The Turkish business context is thus characterized by family ownership, typically in the form of family business groups.[24] State has provided incentives and supported the development of these family business groups by easing their access to finance through equity participations and credits from state banks, supplying low cost inputs, and protecting them from foreign competition.[25] Relations with the state have been vital in gaining access to government contracts and benefiting from opportunities resulting from changing regulations.[26] Significance of the relations with the state has required the owning families to be active in the management of their companies and to carefully handle the intricate relationships with the State.[27] Thus, the requirements of the relations with the state have been one of the important determinants of ownership and governance attributes of businesses in this context. In addition to the support that the state has offered to the family business groups, the state has also acted as a substantial economic player through the state-owned enterprises. State ownership still accounts for a considerable portion of economic activity in spite of the privatizations carried out since the 1980s. Companies owned by municipalities have also emerged as notable economic players after the legislation on local governments. Other nonfamily owner identities include institutional owners, such as pension funds and banks. And another significant ownership identity in this context is foreign ownership. In the following pages, the typical dominant ownership categories are discussed under the headings of business groups (including family- and nonfamily business groups), state ownership, bank ownership, and foreign ownership.

## Business Groups

As collections of industrial and financial firms under a legally organized holding company owning and managing them, business groups are the dominant form of organization of large businesses in the Turkish business context.[28] Similar to other emerging countries, institutional voids resulting from market imperfections[29,30] together with active participation of state in the economic resource allocation[31] reinforced the emergence of business groups as prevalent forms of organization for businesses in Turkey. Business groups provided solutions to the challenges posed by underdeveloped capital markets, scarcity of skilled human capital and management knowhow, and uncertain business environment caused by discretionary and discriminatory state interventions. Several of the prominent business groups started their businesses as early as the 1920s and 1930s.[32] Business groups started organizing as holding companies in the 1960s, after the government abolished the legal structure leading to double taxation of profits transferred from the group company to the parent company.[33] The Koç Holding was the second to adopt the holding structure in 1963 (after the establishment of Yatırımlar Holding following the military coup of 1960[34]) and thus, to become a family business group. It was followed by the Sabancı Holding in 1967. Sakıp Sabancı (one of the Sabancı brothers owning the company) stated that they had transformed their company into a holding since they closely followed the Koç Holding with the assumption that if Vehbi Koç (the founder of the Koç Holding) does it, this must be something good.[35] Since then, holding companies have proliferated and have had a central role in corporate governance in Turkey.

Family ownership and control is a salient attribute of the business groups in Turkey. The majority of large business groups are family owned, except for the special cases such as the İşbank and the Oyak group.[36] The largest 50 economic players in Turkey in 2005, as compiled by Colpan[37] according to the number of employees, include 28 diversified business groups, considering both the private sector businesses and state-owned enterprises, of which 26 of them are family business groups.

Most of the prominent family holding companies, such as the Koç Holding, the Sabancı Holding, the Doğan Holding, and the Eczacıbaşı Holding are traded in the Borsa İstanbul. A considerable number of affiliated companies in these family business groups are also listed. In fact, the two largest and oldest family business groups, the Koç and Sabancı holding companies together with their affiliated listed companies constitute more than a quarter of the total market capitalization in the Borsa İstanbul.[38] Including their holding companies, the numbers of listed companies in the ISE from the Koç and Sabancı groups are, respectively, 16 and 12. Together with the prominent family business groups, the two important nonfamily business groups, İşbank and Oyak, have a marked

*Table 5.2 Major business groups in the Istanbul stock exchange— 2009*

| Business group | # of Listed companies | Avg. group shares | Avg. family members' shares | Avg. free float |
|---|---|---|---|---|
| Koç | 16 | 54.20 | 2.95 | 31.34 |
| bank | 15 | 58.46 | – | 39.17 |
| Sabancı | 12 | 54.13 | 0.00 | 26.63 |
| Doğan | 9 | 62.26 | 1.50 | 27.07 |
| Oyak | 9 | 57.43 | – | 37.88 |
| Anadolu | 6 | 60.65 | 0.00 | 28.10 |
| Ülker | 6 | 49.83 | 9.96 | 39.96 |
| Yaşar | 6 | 65.22 | 0.00 | 29.79 |
| Doğuş | 5 | 40.71 | 0.01 | 48.04 |
| Eczacıbaşı | 5 | 61.84 | 0.00 | 38.16 |
| Akkök | 4 | 40.29 | 1.56 | 40.91 |
| Alarko | 3 | 55.16 | 24.24 | 30.83 |
| İhlas | 3 | 23.19 | 3.69 | 76.02 |
| Metro | 3 | 33.95 | 17.57 | 66.04 |
| Polat | 3 | 64.57 | 3.65 | 35.43 |
| Zorlu | 3 | 63.08 | 0.00 | 35.92 |

Source: Yamak and Ertuna (2010).[39]

presence in the Borsa İstanbul, with 15 and 9 companies, respectively, trading in the ISE as of the end of 2015.

Considering all the companies listed in the Borsa İstanbul in 2009, there are more than 100 business groups, represented by 237 companies out of a total of 315 listed companies. Sixteen of these business groups have three or more companies listed in the exchange, representing a total of 108 companies. The list of these business groups, together with the number and ownership structures of their listed companies, is presented in Table 5.2.

Out of the 16 business groups, represented with three or more companies in the ISE, 14 of them are family owned, while the remaining two are a bank and a pension fund. Concentrated ownership is commonly observed in the listed companies belonging to these large business groups, indicated by a high average percentage of group shares in companies belonging to a given group. In most of the business groups (11 out of 16), average group shares in the affiliated companies is more than 50 percent. Average shares of dispersed owners in business group companies are comparable to that of the total companies in the exchange.

## Family Business Groups

Research confirms that families maintain control over their companies by holding concentrated ownership structures, usually organized under a business group, with family members actively involved in both the strategic and the operational decisions of their companies.[40] Considering family business groups with the highest number of listed group companies in 2009, the average group share ownership percentage is over 50 percent.[41] Family groups are controlled by a single family such as the Koç Group or a coalition composed of a small number of families[42,43] such as the Anadolu Group. Business groups have centralized management systems, and control is maintained by a central management unit where key managerial positions are held by the founding family members, even in the case of large listed companies of family business groups.[44] Other mechanisms used by families to maintain control over their group companies are pyramidal structures,[45] interlocking directorates across group companies,[46] and cross-shareholdings.[47] Boards of the family business group companies are typically dominated by insiders, with a low representation of out-siders in the board,[48,49] and qualification of retired employees as outside board members.[50] Family members are significantly represented in the boards of their holding companies and affiliated group companies. The percentage of family members in the boards of the holding companies of the largest Turkish family business groups reach as high as 40 percent.[51] The chairman position in the boards of both the holding company and the affiliated companies in the family business groups are often held by family members,[52] but this duality is not a commonly observed feature in the boards and chairman, with chief executive officers (CEOs) usually being different persons in the listed family group companies.[53] CEOs are not as powerful as their counterparts in countries with dispersed ownership structures, and some of the CEOs of listed companies of family business groups were not even board members until recently.[54]

There are indications of increased professionalism in family business groups. The number of professional managers in boards is increasing, at the detriment of family members.[55] Additionally, direct shareholdings of fam-ily members in the affiliated companies of family business groups are also decreasing.[56] In fact, the average percentage of shares held by individual family members decreased from 12 to 9.6 percent in the ISE listed com-panies, displaying a 2.4 percent decrease from 1999 to 2009.[57] Ownership by individual family members is less common in companies belonging to a family business group. In 11 of the 14 family business groups listed in Table 5.2, individual family members have negligible direct ownership stakes in their group companies. The average ownership stakes of indi-vidual family members is 4.8 percent in the affiliated companies of the 14 family business groups. Rather than owning direct ownership stakes in the affiliated companies of their family business groups, individual family members have ultimate controlling shares through their investments in their holding companies or the unlisted companies having majority control in their holding companies. Despite the indications of increased professionalism in management positions and in board structure, dom-ination of controlling families still continues. Families maintain their dominance by both collectively holding the majority of the shares and utilizing additional mechanisms such as unofficial family committees or working groups, functioning alongside the formal institutionalized boards in their companies and giving the strategic decisions for the total group.[58] Continuing domination of families is a feature attributable to both the old family business groups founded before 1980s as well as the new family business groups.[59] Board structure of listed companies in Turkey is largely uniform, and there are no significant differences between family and nonfamily companies, except for CEO tenure and director compensation, according to a study on 303 companies out of which 142 are family owned and 84 are nonfamily owned.[60] Oba et al. find that CEO tenure is longer and directors are paid more in family companies, commenting that longer CEO tenure and higher director compensation contribute to the strengthening family dominance by supporting entrenchment.

Most of the family business groups are diversified conglomerates, consisting of companies operating in a wide range of unrelated industries with vertically centralized control structures.[61] This form of organization offers significant benefits in a context characterized by market failures together with uncertainties and opportunities caused by the state. However, economic reasons are not sufficient in elucidating the widespread existence of family business groups. Family business groups are also "social" establishments,[62] serving social functions that are important acts in an emerging economy, such as establishing schools, universities, hospitals, museums, and cultural centers. In fact, most of the family business groups organize these activities through the charitable foundations of their controlling families[63] in the form of corporate social responsibility. Companies in the group make donations to the foundations of the controlling families and report the activities of the foundation as their corporate social responsibility practices. This practice is evaluated as a governance issue in a report by the Organization for Economic Cooperation and Development (OECD[64]) on the assessment of the corporate governance environment in Turkey. The OECD acknowledges that it is common practice for companies in Turkey to pursue noncommercial activities, which are in the form of social causes supported by philanthropic foundations of the controlling owners, additionally finding the transparency of the decision processes regarding these noncommercial activities to be inadequate.

Most of the early family business groups that survived are in their third generation and families maintain collective control. However, difficulties in maintaining control and keeping the family together pose potential governance issues for family business groups. In fact, in the Sabancı Holding, one of the oldest and largest family groups in Turkey, a second-generation family member left the group to have his own conglomerate.[65] Conflicts of interests between family members, especially among those who are in control and those who are left out, appear as vital governance challenges for family business groups. The Uzel Holding, which was one of the oldest family business groups with an agricultural machinery manufacturing company ranking among the world's top 10, collapsed due to governance issues over a family dispute. Having no heir to entrust the group also poses a significant challenge for the continuity family business groups. An innovative governance model was implemented by the founder of the Elginkan Group, as he transformed the group into one that is exclusively owned by a charitable foundation, controlled by a board of trustees composed of diverse stakeholders.[66] According to the foundation voucher of the Elginkan Foundation,[67] its board of trustees includes a wide array of stakeholders including representatives from five of the prominent universities in Turkey, representatives from various institutions such the Scientific and Technological Research Council of Turkey, the Turkish Standards Institution, the Manisa Municipality, the Metal Industrialists Union, the Turkish Armed Forces Foundation, and the İş Bank. A family business group has thus been transformed by its founder before his death into a nonfamily business group, owned and controlled solely by a charitable trust foundation. Charitable trust foundation is a common practice among the Turkish business groups. Vehbi Koç, the founder of the Koç Group states in his biography that foundations may help the company survive through generations.[68,69]

Given the fact that the business context of Turkey is dominated by family business groups, innovative structures, and mechanisms for keeping the families together or planning succession seem to be crucial for long-term viability.

## Nonfamily Business Groups

In the landscape of large businesses in Turkey, there are also nonfamily business groups owned predominantly by institutional owners such as political parties, armed forces, and charitable foundations. Among the listed companies, the İş Bank and the Oyak group are the two prominent nonfamily business groups in Turkey.

### The İş Bank Group

İş Bank (literally meaning "Business Bank") is the first private capital bank founded in 1924, a year after the establishment of the Republic of Turkey. The founders of the bank included tradesmen, members of the parliament, and influential politicians who had participated in the War of Independence. The bank was established with the aim of encouraging new businesses that would be established and managed by Turkish businessmen under the strong protection of the state, thereby aiming to facilitate the development of a national private sector. In a way, the İş Bank was established to act as a mechanism for integrating the state and the private sector. Considering the characteristics of its founding team and its mission, İş Bank appears like a state bank, though it is in fact a private bank, established as a corporation under the commercial law.[70] The İş Bank became the leading institution to support private enterprises through both participating in their equity and providing credits. Equity participations of İş Bank were mostly in sectors protected by the state through state-created monopolies, such as mining, sugar, textiles, and insurance.[71] These equity participations formed the basis of the large business group today. Since its inception, İş Bank has participated in the equity of 293 companies and has sold its participation in 268 of these companies. By 2015, the İş Bank group consists of 25 directly controlled and 88 indirectly controlled companies operating in finance, glass, telecommunications, and manufacturing and services industries.[72]

The İş Bank has an unusual ownership structure. Employees' retirement fund and a political party own the majority of the shares in İş Bank. The shares of Mustafa Kemal Atatürk, the founder of the Republic of Turkey, were turned over to the Republican People's Party (CHP), and dividend incomes of these shares were then donated to the Turkish Linguistics Society and the Turkish History Institute, at the request of Atatürk as stated in his will. Thus, the single party, which was at the power during the establishment of the republic and which is currently the main opposition party in the National Assembly, owns a significant portion of the shares. The breakdown of ownership in İş Bank is as follows: the retirement fund of İş Bank employees owns 40 percent, while 28 percent of shares belong to the CHP, and the remaining 32 percent is in free float.

There are 15 companies in the Borsa İstanbul, owned and controlled directly or indirectly by İş Bank. This group of companies is one of the prominent groups in the Borsa İstanbul. The market value of the 15 listed İş Bank group companies is around 7.6 percent of the total market value of ISE by 2015.[73] None of the companies in the group owns shares in the parent company İş Bank. As displayed in Table 5.2, the average share of İş Bank group in its 15 listed companies is 58.5 percent, while the average share of free float is 39.2 percent, indicating a highly concentrated ownership structure in the listed İş Bank group of companies.

*Oyak Group: Pension Fund*

OYAK (Ordu Yardımlaşma Kurumu—Turkish Armed Forces Assistance Fund) is one of the important nonfamily business groups in Turkey. It was incorporated in 1961 by a special law (Law No. 205)[74] with the purpose of providing the members of the Turkish Armed Forces a variety of financial support services such as loans, retirement income, death benefits, and disability benefits. The company identifies itself as a private legal entity in the form of a pension fund committed to achieve the highest return for its members from its investments in affiliated companies and financial investments. The special law on the establishment of OYAK clearly defines the governing bodies, their composition, duties of the board, and mechanisms of control, as well as membership status, revenues, management of its assets, and services to be given the Fund. As such, the law corresponds to an article of association in a company. OYAK has no shareholders, but members. The number of the members of the fund, including both permanent and temporary members, is 291,618 by the end of 2014.[75] All officers and military employees of the Turkish Armed Forces are the permanent members, and those who conduct active military service are the temporary members. The fund respectively receives 10 and 5 percent membership fees from the salaries of the permanent and temporary members and invests them in a wide array of 70 companies in manufacturing, services, and finance industries.

The group of companies is managed by professional managers after the restructuring program of OYAK in 2001. According to the Law, the governance and control structure of the group is dominated by military officers, while military personnel do not occupy the management positions of OYAK group of companies.[76] The top management team of the business group has become professional during the restructuring program, which started after the hiring of Coşkun Ulusoy as the general manager.[77] Ulusoy, who still continues to serve in this position, has received his PhD degree in the United States. He previously worked in the general manager positions in the two largest state banks. The top management team he has formed during the restructuring program included well-known professionals from prominent companies in Turkey. The group has a unique structure of governance and control as top military officials, ministers from state, high-ranking government officials, and members of industry associations are included in the governing bodies and committees. Very little has been researched in the relevant academic literature on the governance mechanisms specific to the OYAK group of companies, but in the management review of performance, the success of the specific model of converting small savings into long-term large investments has been attributed to the structure of ownership, management, and control.[78] As of the end of 2014, the group has more than 28,000 employees.[79] In the 500 Largest Industrial Organizations of Turkey drawn up by the Istanbul Chamber of Industry,[80] a list defining size based on sales revenue of manufactured goods, there are three OYAK group of companies in the top 10 in 2014, namely the Oyak-Renault ranking the third, the İskenderun Iron and Steel Co., and Ereğli Iron Steel Co., ranking seventh and eighth, respectively. The OYAK group also has an important presence in the cement industry. There are six large cement producing companies are in the OYAK group. The companies owned and managed by the OYAK group are not confined to Turkey, with the group having investments in 16 different countries including various European countries, Russia, Brasilia, and China.[81] Out of the 70 companies directly or indirectly owned by the group, 9 are listed in the ISE. In these companies, the average share ownership by OYAK is

57.4 percent, while dispersed shares average 39.2 percent as of the end of 2009, as displayed in Table 5.2.

### State Ownership

Despite the fact that the role of state as an economic actor has decreased following the privatization program which started in the 1990s, the state is still a determining economic actor of the Turkish business context. In the state-dependent system of Turkey, state influence on the economy is exercised both through state-desired allocations and state-owned enterprises, although state ownership is decreasing in magnitude. In her study on business groups in Turkey, Colpan[82] depicts the large enterprise landscape of Turkey as a two-pillar economy composed of diversified business groups and state-owned enterprises. In the list of 50 largest economic players in 2005, compiled by Colpan based on the number of employees as an indicator of size, 18 of the largest economic players are state-owned enterprises. State-owned enterprises in this list are operating in a wide range of manufacturing and service industries, including both old and new economy companies. The list includes economic entities operating in manufacturing goods such as sugar, tea, salt, tobacco and tobacco products, alcoholic and nonalcoholic beverages, industrial machinery, military weapons and systems, coal mining, power generation; and in services such as electricity distribution, transportation services, including railways, aviation and airport services, postal services, financial services, and banking services. However, some of these state-owned enterprises have been largely or partially privatized since 2005, while a number of companies are in the privatization process and are currently included in the portfolio of the Prime Ministry Privatization Administration.[83]

Among the 500 Largest Industrial Organizations identified by the Istanbul Chamber of Industry, there are 11 state-owned enterprises in 2014. This number corresponds to a significant decrease in the presence of state-owned enterprises among the largest industrial companies, considering the fact that there were 66 state-owned companies in the same list in 1993. The number can be expected to decrease further as 3 state-owned companies among the 11 in the list are also among the portfolio of companies to be privatized.[84] This list is compiled according to sales revenue as the indicator of size. State-owned companies in the largest industrial companies list operate in electricity production, mining, oil, coal, locomotive, military weapons and systems, tea, sugar, and meat, and dairy products manufacturing industries. There is a large discrepancy with respect to the size of these companies, as the largest state-owned company (Elektrik Üretim A.Ş. Genel Müdürlüğü-EÜAŞ, General Directorate of Electric Production Co.) generates a sales volume of 6.7 billion TL, ranking the 5th largest industrial company, while the smallest state-owned company (Türkiye Lokomotif ve Motor San. A.Ş, Turkish Locomotive and Motor Industry Co.) in the list generates 264 million TL in annual sales revenue, ranking the 401th. State-owned companies in the 500 Largest Industrial Organizations List for 2014[85] together with their respective rankings and sales volumes are presented in Table 5.3.

State-owned companies do not generally operate under market conditions. EÜAŞ, the largest state-owned company in the 500 Largest

Table 5.3 *State-owned companies in 500 largest industrial organizations in Turkey—2014*

| | Ranking in 2014 | Sales revenue (TL)* |
|---|---|---|
| EÜAŞ General Directorate of Electric Production Co. | 5 | 6,707,382,164 |
| Turkish Sugar Factories Co. | 19 | 3,085,712,484 |
| Turkish Petroleum Corporation | 25 | 2,482,372,036 |
| Eti General Directorate of Mining Plants | 41 | 1,974,517,342 |
| Not disclosed | 43 | n.a. |
| The General Directorate of Tea Plants | 44 | 1,901,964,981 |
| Soma Electric Production and Commerce Co. | 108 | 808,522,103 |
| The General Directorate of Mechanical and Chemical Industry Corporation | 139 | 658,228,300 |
| The General Directorate of Meat and Milk Authority | 160 | 590,950,562 |
| The General Directorate of Turkish Hardcoal Authority | 379 | 279,316,348 |
| Turkish Locomotive and Motor Industry Co. (TÜLOMSAŞ) | 401 | 264,204,293 |

Source: Compiled by the authors, (*) USD/TL exchange rate is 2.32 as of the end of 2014.

Industrial Organizations list, ranks the 27th in the 50 Largest Economic Actors List compiled by Colpan,[86] a list prepared as based on the number of employees as an indicator of size. This electricity-producing company has only two customers, which are also state-owned companies. Even though the company is under a significant restructuring program due to the changes in the electricity market regulations,[87] it operates in a different realm regarding the principles of corporate governance. In fact, very little is publicly disclosed with respect to their corporate governance structures. Despite the unique features of the supervision of assets, internal control, stakeholder involvement due to inherent presence of the potential for political intervention and extraction, there is scarce academic research into the corporate governance principles, structures, and mechanisms employed in state-owned companies in Turkey.

More is disclosed on corporate governance in publicly listed state-owned companies, which have been exposed to market discipline to a certain degree. As a result of the ongoing implementation of privatization policy, shareholdings of the state or state-related institutions in publicly listed companies are decreasing. The number of state-owned and controlled companies is 14 as of 2009, with the state having a majority ownership in 7 of these companies.[88] By 2015, minority shares of the state in two of these state-owned companies have been privatized, while three are now in the privatization portfolio of the Privatization Administration.[89] Two of the three companies in the privatization portfolio are the Halk Bank, a large state-owned bank, and the Turkish Airlines, in which the Privatization Administration owns, respectively, 75.03 and 49.12 percent of the shares.

### Bank Ownership

Banks do not appear as major shareholders in the ownership structure of companies in Turkey.[90] A significant exception is the case of İş Bank, which is one of the nonfamily business groups in Turkey. This bank, the largest private retail bank with 1,341 branches all over Turkey and abroad,[91] has equity participations and is the parent company of the İş Bank group of companies. Except for the case of İş Bank, banks do not generally have equity participations in other companies, though banks are the dominant players in financial markets as financial intermediaries and as major source credits for industrial companies. Hence, banks in Turkey do not pursue governance tasks as their counterparts do in Japan and Germany, in the form of offering or coordinating support in crisis situations or assisting effective mobilization of dispersed shareholdings via deposited voting rights.[92] On the other hand, most of the largest business groups include banks in their group of companies; so, many banks are owned and controlled by large business groups.[93] For instance, the Koç Group has a controlling stake in Yapı Kredi Bank, through a joint venture with Unicredit. Other business groups such as Doğuş, Fiba, and Sabancı control their affiliated banks, respectively, Garanti Bank, Fibabank, Akbank, either alone or with their partners. However, the number of family business groups possessing a bank decreased following the financial crisis of 2001. For example, Doğan Holding's Dışbank was sold to Fortis, which later became TEB following a merger with the BNP. Similarly, Cıngıllı Holding's Demirbank was bought by the HSBC. Additionally, banks received significant amount of foreign equity participations during the 2000s.

### Foreign Ownership

Foreign ownership is a marked attribute of the Turkish business landscape, with significant foreign ownership mostly in the form of institutional investors in publicly listed companies.[94] The ISE were exposed to foreign portfolio investments in 1989 and foreign investors have been important actors in the market since then. The share of foreign investors fluctuates around two-thirds, in which institutional investors have a significant share. According to the records of the Central Registration Agency, the share of foreign portfolio investors in free float was 65.1 percent by the end of 2006, out of which 42.1 percent belonged to foreign institutional investors, corresponding to 27.4 percent of free float. There are also large multinational, foreign-owned companies among the publicly listed companies.[95] As of the end of 2012, foreign investors' share in free float is around two-thirds according to a report by the OECD.[96] Compared to other emerging markets, the share of foreign institutions in free float is large, considering the results of a 29-country study, in which Turkey ranks the second highest.[97]

There are also large multinational companies in listed companies in the Borsa Istanbul. Both the number and the amount of foreign investment increased considerably after the 2001 financial crisis, as foreign investors acquired many companies that became financially distressed due to the crisis. While there were only 14 publicly listed companies where more than 50 percent of the shares were held by foreign investors in 1999, there were 38 such companies in 2009.[98] With respect to companies with foreign equity, the average foreign shareholding increased from 35 percent in 1999 to 53 percent in 2009 in listed companies in the Borsa Istanbul. Foreign investors have varying degrees of shares in companies, which can be classified as foreign majority ownership, equal share ownership between domestic and foreign investors and minority foreign ownership. The type of their equity configurations appears to have a series of consequences with regard to the governance mechanisms foreign investors utilize, which in turn influence their performance results.[99] Foreign majority, equal share, and foreign minority configurations of foreign ownership display distinct ownership and corporate governance characteristics, which influence their ability to meet the requirements of the institutional context and their performance. Best performance relates to the equal share configuration, which seem to better address contextual uncertainties and eliminate consequences of liability of foreignness through enabling access to context-specific knowledge and networks, and to incentives and privileges provided through their joint venture partners' political connections. In fact, some large multinational companies such as the Ford Company, the Fiat, or the Bridgestone have formed joint ventures on an equal share basis with large family business groups in Turkey. Equal share configuration appears to be attractive for the foreign investors as this configuration decreases the risk of expropriation through better monitoring of the local partner, while offering better adaption to the requirements of the institutional context.

It is worth noting that foreign investors prefer family business groups, who are, as mentioned earlier, the main actors of the business context in Turkey. Similarly, foreign institutional investors seem to prefer companies with family control,[100] which is a finding contrary to most of prior research in this area. There might be two reasons for this: lower potential for expropriation by family companies due to relatively low wedge between cash flow rights and control rights or higher potential for controlling families to enter into informal contracts with foreign institutional investors in order to increase their investor base in the absence of domestic institutional investors. It is indeed observed that foreign investors entering into partnership with companies that are affiliated with a family business group perform better.[101]

There has been a significant inflow of foreign equity into the banking sector during the 2000s, especially following the banking sector reform implemented after the 2001 financial crisis in Turkey. This period witnessed foreign equity participations in banks possessed by prominent family business groups, such as the Koç, Sabancı, and Doğuş groups. Foreign equity participations into the banks in Turkey in the 2000s are compiled in Table 5.4.

Some of these banks have experienced further changes in their ownership structure. For example, TEB and Fortis merged. In the case of the Garanti Bank, Banco Bilbao Vizcaya Argentaria (BBVA) bought the shares of the GE Consumer Finance and the Doğuş Group; and

*Table 5.4 Foreign equity purchases of banks in Turkey between 2005 and 2007*

| Bank | Year of purchase | Foreign investor | Percentage share (%) | Amount paid by foreign investors |
|---|---|---|---|---|
| TEB | 2005 | BNP Paribas | 42.1 | $217 mil. |
| Fortis (Dışbank) | 2005 | Fortis | 89.5 | 985 mil. |
| Garanti | 2005 | GE Consumer Finance | 26.0 | $1,550 mil. |
| Yapı Kredi | 2005 | Unicredito | 57.0 | 1,182 mil. |
| Finansbank | 2006 | National Bank | 46.0 | 2,300 mil. |
| Denizbank | 2006 | Dexia | 75.0 | $2,437 mil. |
| Şekerbank | 2006 | Bank Turan-Alem | 34 | $255 mil. |
| Akbank | 2006 | Citigroup | 20 | $3,100 mil. |
| Tekfenbank | 2007 | Eurobank EFG | 70 | $182 mil. |
| Oyakbank | 2007 | ING Bank | 100 | $2,673 mil. |

*Source:* Compiled by the authors.

as of 2015, it became the major shareholder by holding 39.9 percent of the shares.[102] As a result, the Doğuş Group's shares were reduced to 6.19 percent. Moreover, the Denizbank, which was sold to the Dexia, was finally bought by the Russian Sberbank in 2012. Furthermore, in the case of Şekerbank, the Samruk-Kazyna Sovereign Wealth Fund, BTA Securities, and International Finance Corporation became Şekerbank's partners. Other banks undergoing a change in their ownership structure were the Akbank and the Eurobank Tekfen. The GE Consumer Finance sold off its shares in the Akbank, thus leaving the Sabancı Holding as the sole block holder. At the Eurobank Tekfen, a Kuwait-based financial services group, the Burgan Bank, acquired the company in 2012.[103]

## Owner Activism

Takeover risks are minimal due to the concentrated ownership structure commonly observed in this context. In a context characterized by weak investor protection, shareholders hold concentrated ownership structures in response to the constraints posed by the legal and regulatory weaknesses. In most cases, it is impossible to acquire a firm without the consent of the controlling shareholder. Thus, market does not have a disciplining effect on low performance, so an active market for corporate control does not exist in Turkey.[104]

Investor base is limited in Turkey, with domestic institutional investors having a scant presence. The share of domestic institutional investors have less than one percent ownership stake in the listed manufacturing companies considering the period between 1999 and 2000. Similarly, the average share of domestic institutional investors in free float is 1.1 percent as of the end of 2006, considering a sample including ISE-100 companies.[105] Introduction of a private pension incentive scheme by the government in 2012 is expected to promote private savings and increase domestic institutional investments.[106] In the absence of domestic institutional investors, controlling shareholders have no option but foreign institutional investors in order to expand their investor base. According to the share level data provided by the Central Registry Agency, the share of foreign institutional investors in free float is 27.4 percent by the end of 2006. Although it can be argued that the level of shares held by foreign institutional investors in a company is too small to bear the cost of monitoring,[107] findings on better transparency and voluntary information disclosure in companies with higher foreign institutional investment suggest for the presence of a monitoring role by foreign institutional investors. Given the limited investor base, companies can adopt better corporate governance mechanisms in order to eliminate the constraints posed by the legal and regulatory institutional context to attract foreign institutional investors. This might be a contributing factor for the relatively high presence of foreign institutional investors in the market.

# CHAPTER 6

# Boards of Directors in the Turkish Economy

## Board Structure

In Turkey, corporate boards are single-tier and there is an insider controlled corporate governance system.[1] A study conducted among companies in the ISE 50 index reports the average number of directors to be 8.5.[2] However, in a recent study on listed nonfinancial firms' boards, the average board size is found to be six for both family and nonfamily firms.[3] Board size seems to change depending on the industry in question. For example, in the financial sector, the average number of the directors in the boardroom is found to be 8.5, while this figure for manufacturing and service sectors are, respectively, 7.7 and 7.2.[4] With the existence of a joint venture, board size tends to increase.[5] In some joint ventures, where equity is equally shared with a foreign partner, both parties usually prefer to have equal number of directors, which thus leads to larger boards.[6] In the Ford Automotive Industry Co. (a joint venture of the Koç Holding with the Ford Motor Company) there are 14 directors; half of whom are foreigners and half of whom Turkish. Even the "independent" directors are selected according to this equity rule: one foreigner, one Turkish.[7] In other foreign-owned companies, there are usually foreign directors representing the equity but also Turkish directors familiar with the Turkish context. For instance, board size adds up to 12 directors in the Albaraka Turk Bank with 6 foreign directors.

Larger firms are inclined to have larger boards and board committees. The largest Turkish company (in terms of net sales),[8,9] TÜPRAŞ has 15 board members.[10] Most of them are Koç family members and current/previous managers of Koç Holding owning the company. TÜPRAŞ has four committees namely, audit, corporate governance, risk management, and finally ethics. Turkish Airlines, ranking 4th in the largest 500 companies in Turkey according to *Fortune*, has nine board members and three committees on audit, corporate governance, and early risk assessment. On the other hand, other largest state-owned enterprises such as TCDD (railways), TETAŞ (electricity), and PTT (postal services) have all smaller boards. Although these institutions (TCDD,[11,12] TETAŞ,[13] and PTT[14]) are among the largest Turkish enterprises, they have relatively small board sizes (5, 4, and 5 respectively) and only an ethics committee.

The Capital Market Board (CMB) recommends the establishment of audit and corporate governance committee. A study carried out among the ISE 50 index companies reveals that while 48 companies (out of 50) have audit committees, only 27 had a corporate governance committee.[15] Among the nonfinancial listed companies, the percentage of family owned companies and nonfamily owned companies possessing only the audit committee is found to be 55 and 64 percent; and those also having a corporate governance committee is, respectively, 27 and 20 percent.[16] Yet, according to the same study, 12 percent of family firms and 3 percent of nonfamily firms have no committees.

The CMB requires the committees to be majorly composed of nonexecutive directors and to be led by independent directors. However, among the ISE 50 index companies,[17] only 11 had an independent director heading the audit committee and 10 with a corporate governance committee led by an independent director. In 30 companies, there were no independent directors in the committees. Only in 34 over 50 companies was the audit committee largely composed of nonexecutive directors. The chairman- and chief executive officer (CEO)-led committees are not uncommon.

In addition to regular public and private companies, there are also particular companies with different ownership and governance structures. For example, OYAK (Ordu Yardımlaşma Kurumu—Turkish Armed Forces Assistance Fund) constitutes one of the largest nonfamily business groups manufacturing, among others, 43 percent of automobiles, 16 percent of cement, and 67 percent of flat steel in Turkey.[18] The company is a private legal entity in the form of pension fund for armed forces, being subject to the special OYAK law for its governance.[19]

There is a multilevel governance structure composed of hierarchical committees controlling the board of directors and management. Top military officials, ministers, high-ranking government officials, and members of the industry associations take part in the governing bodies and committees. According to the law, the board is composed of seven members and the general manager is its member. Three of the directors are from the armed forces, who are nominated by the Ministry of Defense and the Office of Commander-in-Chief. The remaining four are required to have a background in banking, insurance, finance, or law; and they are selected by a committee composed of Ministers of the Financial Affairs and Defense, high-ranking government officials, and heads of industry associations. The same committee also selects the chairman.

Another interesting structure is observed in Elginkan owned by a charitable foundation that is controlled by a board of trustees. This innovative self-governance model was adopted by the founder of the group who had wanted to insure the survival of the family business, thereby transforming it into a foundation. According to the Foundation Voucher,[20] its board of trustees includes a wide array of stakeholders including representatives from five of the prominent universities in Turkey, representatives from various institutions such as the Scientific and the Technological Research Council of Turkey, the Turkish Standards Institution, the Manisa Municipality, the Metal Industrialists Union, the Turkish Armed Forces Foundation, and the İş Bank. Finally, some members are selected by the group companies. The board of directors can be composed of either seven or nine members. Board of trustees must select five of seven or six of nine directors among the members of the board of trustees by secret ballot.

### Board Composition

According to the Turkish Commercial Law, the board of directors is composed of one or more persons who are appointed either by the articles of association or elected by general assembly in joint stock companies.[21] And according to the new Commercial Code, the legal entities are also allowed to become members of the board by a representative.

The state-dependent nature of the Turkish business system leads to a dominant organization form, namely the family business group form, a factor also having important repercussions on its board composition. The low level of interpersonal trust prevailing in Turkey together with the necessity of careful handling of intricate relations between the state and businessmen induce the founder and his/her descendants to act as board members and managers in family business groups (FBGs). The percentage of family board members can be as high as 40 percent in the largest FBGs.[22] It is worth noting that the number of professional managers is increasing at the detriment of family directors[23] in the boardroom of FBGs. However, these are trusted professional managers who have long tenures in the company, thus being able to enhance insider domination and family control.[24] A similar tendency is also observed in interlocking directorship in the affiliates. The use of interlocking directors is one of the internal control mechanisms shaping the board composition especially in FBGs.[25] Family members and insider professionals constituted 70 percent of board members in affiliated companies in 2002.[26] In a study[27] that Ataay conducted among 331 companies in the Borsa İstanbul, she found interlocking ties in 184 companies (269 out of 2,036 directors). She claims that 82 percent of the directorates take place within the family owned and managed enterprises. It is very rare to find interlocks between different FBGs.[28] Interlocks are more intragroup than intergroup. So there is more competition rather than collaboration among the FBGs. Therefore, interlocks being intragroup in nature, they are not common (around 12.7 percent) among nonrelated companies, and about 75 percent of the interlocks take place within the same business group.[29] Horizontal interlocks occurring among the affiliates of the related companies are common according to Ataay.[30] She reports the percentage of horizontal interlocks to be 66 percent in total interlocks, 56 percent within business groups, and finally 55 percent in FBGs. Since 42.7 percent of the companies sharing the same directors operate in the same sector, the interlocks can be thought as sharing of industry-specific knowledge along within-group coordination.[31]

There is an insider domination in the boards. The family members, managers of the affiliated companies, retired managers, and current managers constitute, respectively, about 19.3, 46.8, 4.9, and 9 percent of each board in a sample of 299 FBG-affiliated companies.[32] In another study[33] carried out among the ISE 100 index companies, it is found out that family linked directors constituted, respectively, 18.34 and 17.86 percent in 2006 and 2008. Employees' ratio among directors increased from an initial 40.19 percent in 2006 to 41.21 percent in 2008. As these studies manifest, nonexecutive directors constitute the majority. They reach 90 percent in the FBG boards, and in only one out of two companies there is an executive director.[34] Another study conducted among the non-financial companies in the Borsa İstanbul points out that nonexecutive directors constitute the majority in the boardroom, both in family and nonfamily firms, that is, in 67 percent of family firms and 71 percent of nonfamily firms. Although there seems to be a domination of nonexecutive directors, it is also reported that these directors are inclined to fulfill executive tasks, such as the implementation of the strategy.[35]

There is a low representation of outsiders,[36] which is reported to be around 11 percent.[37] On average, 5 percent of each board is found to be composed of outsiders in FBGs.[38] Üsdiken and Yildirim state that almost all the outsiders in their sample are male (except one) and Turkish citizens (except two). The lack of diversity and internationalization is worth noting among the outsiders whose average age is reported to be around 62.[39] Retired employees often appear as outsiders.[40] The civil servants from the bureaucracy constitute one-quarter of all outsiders.[41] In a study on the ISE 100[42] index companies, the ratio of the directors with a background in military is reported to increase from 10.07 percent in 2006 to 11.82 percent in 2008. A similar rise is also observed among directors with a background in politics (from 2.54 to 3.51 percent). Therefore, establishing links with the state apparatus, army, and politics seems to be important for an outsider position.[43] However, it is also interesting to note that chairmen from politics are found to negatively affect risk return efficiency in the banking sector.[44] Having a background in a foreign company also appears to be another sought for characteristic.

Similar to the case of outsiders, the ratio of independent directors is also very limited. In Turkey, public authorities are engaged in the appointment process for independent directors since 2011, when the CMB required that listed companies (other than those in the Watch List

and the Emerging Companies market) hire independent directors fulfilling the prerequisites regarding their qualification and independence. In
the companies with a large market cap and free float value, the board of
directors in collaboration with the nomination committee provides the
CMB with a list of candidates before the general shareholder meeting.[45]
In order to be nominated as independent directors, the candidates must
have the approval of the CMB, which is authorized to perform a detailed
investigation of the proposed candidates, and/or nominate someone for
the independent director position. Besides independence, the nominees
are also evaluated on the basis of qualitative criteria such as having:

1. The necessary educational background, information and experience
   for fulfilling independent director duties.
2. The ethical standards, reputation, and experience enabling the
   independent director to contribute to company activities, protect
   his impartiality with regard to conflict of interest that may arise
   among shareholders, and make independent decisions by taking into
   account the rights of stakeholders.[46]

Therefore, the assessment and the nomination of independent directors are more complicated. Within the limited pool of individuals having
the prerequisites to step in as an independent director, personal contacts
become critical.[47] For example, controlling shareholder usually nominates
directors including the independent ones. While the CMB requires that
the independent members make up one-third of all board members, it is
found that the average percentage of independent members in the boardroom is 15 percent for family firms and 13 percent for nonfamily firms
among nonfinancial quoted companies.[48] Furthermore, the large majority
of the firms (73 percent of family firms and 76 percent of nonfamily firms)
do not have any independent directors. A recent study on 417 listed companies by Ararat, Alkan, and Aytekin shows that the ratio of independent
directors among all board members has reached 28.8 percent in 2015.

The lack of independent directors is more pronounced in state enterprises. Directors usually have a background in other institutions and state
enterprises. Advisors of ministers (see e.g., the PTT) are situated among
the directors. The imprinting effect of politics or the primacy of political

connections is significant in these enterprises, which have a capacity to shape the structures and strategies without leaving much room for monitoring.

Last but not the least, diversity in the boardroom seems to be very limited. Women constituted only around 7 percent of the directors in Turkey in 2006.[49] Although this ratio was very low, it was higher than that of many of the developed countries such as Germany, Spain, Switzerland, Ireland, and Italy. Recent studies on listed companies reveal that the ratio of women directors increased from 9.58 in 2008[50] to 12.9 in 2015.[51] The CMB recommends that the companies target at least 25 percent for female participation in the boardroom. Interesting to note is that companies, fully or partially owned by foreign investors, seem to be more inclined to have female professional managers and directors. For example, Marshall, as a foreign partnership, has a female independent director, namely Yeşim Uçtum. Denizbank, a Russian investment in origin, also has a female director. The Austrian OVM Petroleum Office also has one acting as a chairperson.

Furthermore, foreign directors are not common either. The average of foreign directors is found to be 0.65 percent among the listed manufacturing companies in 2003.[52] The percentage of the equity held by the foreign partner influences the number of the foreign members in the board room. A recent study shows that the average equity held by foreign owners (not including those in the free float) is 19 percent among listed companies,[53] and that the majority of them do not have a major foreign partner. However, even in the companies fully owned by foreign investors, there are local (Turkish) directors. OVM Petroleum Office has four board members, three of whom are foreign and one is Turkish. In the Al Baraka Bank, 5 out of the 11 directors are Turkish.[54] In Denizbank, which has been acquired by the Sberbank Russia, 9 out of 13 directors are foreigners and the rest are Turkish citizens.[55] It can thus be concluded that foreign involvement leads to diversified boards in terms of gender and nationality.

## Board Leadership

Founders or their descendants occupy the leadership position in the FBGs. The chairman of both the FBG and the affiliated firms are often family members.[56] Yet, this duality is not common in listed companies, with incumbents of chairman and the CEO positions often being different persons.[57] However, a recent study on Turkish business elites shows that even if there is no duality in corporate boards, the chairman is usually very much involved in the strategic decision making in family firms.[58]

CEOs, on the other hand, have a limited power, in comparison with the chairman who has the final say on decisions, especially in family firms and family business groups. They act as an aid to the chairman. They are often called as general manager or head of the executive team.[59] In spite of the problems concerning the power concentration at the top, the lack of duality is still found to be positively influencing firm performance.[60]

Despite the limited number of women directors, they still can reach top positions in the boardroom. In 2015, 26 listed companies (6.2 percent) had a female chairperson in the Borsa İstanbul.[61] Among these 26 chairwomen, 21 were affiliated with the controlling family. For example, one of largest FBGs, the Sabancı Holding is headed by a chairwoman, Güler Sabancı,[62] who is also listed among the strongest women in the world.[63] Sabancı Holding has four woman directors, all of whom are members of the Sabancı family (the third generation). Another chairwoman, Gaye Akçen, is both the chairwoman and the head of executive committee at the Elginkan Group owned by a foundation.[64] Moreover, there are also female chairwomen (five in 2015)[65] not affiliated with the controlling family or shareholder. For instance, Gülsüm Azeri, leads the OVM Petroleum Office,[66] the third largest company in Turkey in terms of net sales according to the *Fortune*'s list.[67] She is not only heading the executive committee, but also is the only Turkish and female member of the board of this completely foreign-owned company. This is one of the interesting cases where a female professional climbed up to the highest position without any family linkages.

## Board Behaviors

According to the Global Competitiveness Report of World Economic Forum, efficacy of the corporate boards in Turkey scored 4.4 over 7 and ranked 79 among 144 countries.[68] Together with the patriarchal culture and high-power distance, the board is a place over which the chairman prevails, rather than a place where discussions take place among equals. The boards in Turkish enterprises seem to rubber-stamp the decisions of the controlling shareholders.[69] Low individualism (by extension, high collectivism) is associated with the principal–steward relationship in the boards.[70] Our interviews with board members in preparing this chapter provided interesting comments for delineating this fact. For example:

> The chairman sits the same place at each meeting. Even if he does not attend the meeting nobody dares sitting there. (Executive board member, male, 53, industrial firm)

So, the power of the chairman is stressed even at his absence. Another quote is from a family firm board member:

> My uncle is the Chairperson of the company. I have many new ideas. However our tradition requires that we obey him. We do what he proposes at the board. (Executive board member, male, 41, industrial firm)

The ultimate decision resides with the family, as the following quote from another study[71] indicates:

> As far as I remember, there is no instance where the board member has changed the decision of the family. Our boards function harmoniously, decisions are always taken unanimously.[72]

Oba, Özsoy, and Atakan investigated the functioning of the boards in family firms and identified the following characteristics:[73] Boards act rather as advisory board for the families owning the company since the decision is already made in the family council. In 52.8 percent of the cases, the agenda is said to be set according to the requests of the chairman and the directors. Board nomination and appointment are decided upon by the family among those who seem to be compatible with the owners. Setting the corporate strategy is listed as the major role of the board (83 percent) and monitoring the CEO or financials is somehow not emphasized by board members (23 percent). These findings may be due to the fact that the chairman is often informally involved in strategic management and execution, and that the CEOs are thus relatively weaker. Moreover, paternalism is an important characteristic of the Turkish business culture, potentially impeding a two-way interaction and open discussion between hierarchical levels including the board.

# CHAPTER 7

# Managers in the Turkish Economy

The number of professional managers increases in line with economic growth. Although strategic management decisions are still largely influenced by founders, owners or family member directors in family businesses, especially in the case of the largest companies' professional managers, form a newly emerging class generally with a limited discretion. The top person leading the company is often called the "general manager" in Turkey. The term *chief executive officer* (*CEO*) has been borrowed from the United States, through the consultancy works of McKinsey in Turkey, and Hasan Güleşçi was the first one to be labelled as such in the Sabancı Holding.[1] Up to then, professional managers at the apex with a similar power spectrum had carried the title of "general manager" or "general coordinator." Therefore, the CEO label was introduced into the Turkish conglomerates (holdings, as they are called in Turkey) in 2000, and it was well received. However, Turkish CEOs or general managers are not as powerful as their counterparts in Anglo-Saxon countries. At the beginning of the 2000s, about half of the general managers did not even have a seat in the boardroom.[2] With the new governance legislation, they are now often in the board room of quoted companies but the level of power is still low. There is a wide discrepancy in the relative position of managers depending on the type of company, sector, and geographical location.

## Selection Processes

The selection processes for top managers exhibit differences in relation to industry, company type and the level of the position. In the small and medium-sized companies, human resource activities are handled within the sphere of "personnel" department or in the general administration units closely linked to accounting and law activities, but in large companies, especially in listed ones, there is a human resources (HR) department. Foreign companies and bigger and older manufacturing firms collaborating with foreign capital tend to implement HR practices such as central job application and selection pools, and competency-based training and promotion mechanisms, as well as standardized performance management systems.[3] They collaborate with HR consultancy companies and head hunters for specific positions while also having their own HR departments.

HR activities and selection processes differ according to the sector in question. For instance, in the banking sector, the selection is made through large-scale written examinations followed by successive interviews. Following the crises, there has been a surplus of qualified managers due to layoffs. This has resulted in longer selection processes in which companies strive to select the best possible candidate not only in terms of professional qualifications but also in terms of compatibility of world views and personalities in order to decrease the risk of turnover. Personality tests, group discussions, case studies, outdoor competitions, and even home visits are some of the methods that companies resort to assess candidates' skills. Selection process may include six to seven stages with a series of interviews. According to Aycan, frequent reliance on one-on-one interviews and social networks in staffing is a reflection of collectivistic culture prevailing in Turkey.[4] She also states that interviews are not structured, and the evaluation is usually affected by the subjective perception and intuition of the interviewer.

In the case of most family business groups, the founder or family managers are influential in the process of the top management staffing of their companies. CEOs are usually promoted from within among the trusted individuals. Personal acquaintances and connections, such as being a high school friend of the owner or recommendations of other trusted colleagues or friends, do shape the selection decisions. Trust is very critical in the selection process. As previously mentioned, trust level is very low in Turkish society. Moreover, the powerful state tradition necessitates intricate relations with state officials and the government for the survival of the company. These two factors together lead to the fact that upper echelons are staffed with trusted individuals. School friends are among the most likely candidates. For example, Hüsnü Özyeğin, one of the most successful businessmen in Turkey, started his career in the Çukurova Holding whose owner was a school friend. The same was true for the first CEO of the Sabancı Holding, Hasan Güleşçi, who was a school friend of the second generation of the Sabancı family. As for the Koç Holding, the largest conglomerate company in Turkey, tenure has primary importance. Until recently, the CEOs of the Koç Group were usually selected among the successful managers who had spent almost all their career in the company. For example, Turgay Durak,[5] the previous CEO of the Koç Holding, had started his career in 1976 as an employee in one of the affiliated companies of the group and became the CEO in 2010. He retired from this position in 2015.[6] The new CEO, Levent Çakıroğlu,[7] represents another top manager pattern of the Koç Group. He started his career as an account expert in the Ministry of Financial Affairs where he later became the Vice President of the Investigative Committee of Financial Crimes. He was transferred in 1998 to private sector as the financial coordinator of the Koç Holding where he has spent the rest of his career. This same pattern has also been observed for the CEO of the Doğuş Holding, Hüsnü Akhan,[8] who had started his career in the Turkish Central Bank. In 2001, he moved to the Doğuş Group as a chief financial officer (CFO), and he later became the CEO in 2005. Since the relations with the government are crucial for the firm's survival and tax penalties are thus used as an interest alignment tool by the former, careers in the Ministry of Financial Affairs appear to be a valuable and attractive asset for top executive or board positions in the private sector. It is also observed that in general "initiative and responsibility taking, team work, conscientiousness and customer orientation" are the most sought-for capabilities for employee level and "risk taking, proactivity, entrepreneurial orientation and performance orientedness" turn out to be relevant solely for the managerial level.[9]

## Compensation Practices—Pay for Performance?

Although information about board compensation is relatively easier to access, the disclosure of top executive remuneration is not a common practice in Turkey, even though the Capital Market Board (CMB) requires that all kind of compensation (salary, incentives, bonuses, perks) to board members and top executives be discussed during the annual shareholders' meeting and announced in the annual report.[10] In the same way, it also demands the official announcement of the compensation policy on the company website. However, companies usually prefer to announce a cumulative amount of compensation in their financial documents and on their website. For instance, Ford Automotive Industry, a joint venture of the Koç Holding with the Ford Motor Company, claims to have paid a total of 6,412,328 TL ($2,374,800) to its general manager, 12 board members, 10 assistant general managers, and 3 directors for the first six months until June 30, 2015.[11] A study on listed companies divulged that monthly compensation decisions regarding the board and the CEO are taken during the annual shareholders' meeting among the listed companies, and that the board compensation is usually within the range of a symbolic 1,500–2,700 TL, while the highest observed is 30,000 TL in family firms and 10,000 TL in non-family ones.[12] Interesting to note is that almost half of the nonfinancial listed companies claim not making any payment to board members. Similar finding was underlined in a previous study,[13] noting the presence of pro-bono directors in the ISE 50 companies. These findings are especially surprising in the case of independent directors, indicating a deficiency in terms of aligning board compensation with the long-term interests of the company and the shareholders. This deficiency is also supported by the finding that most companies pay their directors fixed salaries and do not link compensation to performance. Fixed salaries are also very low as compared with other markets. A considerable number of companies state that they pay the legal minimum monthly salary. This peculiar feature of board compensation is also observed in an earlier assessment of corporate governance environment by the Organization for Economic Cooperation and Development (OECD).[14] OECD also points to the inherent risks in this situation and warns that the companies might find it hard to recruit qualified, independent board members if this practice continues. Yet, a series of interviews made with the heads of management consultancy and executive staffing companies reveal that the payments to the directors may well be above the officially disclosed amounts.[15]

While there is more information available for board compensation, that for top executives is quite limited. Top managers enjoy a high remuneration package in comparison to other managers and employees. There is indeed a high discrepancy between top level managers and employees' compensation packages. Since there is a continuous supply to labor market from business schools and newcomers are satisfied with relatively lower wages, the compensation of lower level employees can hardly reach the standard.[16]

The compensation practices display a large variety depending on the industry, type of company, relationship with the owners, and executive supply conditions of the time. Highest compensation packages are observed in finance, telecommunication, pharmaceuticals, fast-moving consumer goods, logistics, and software sectors. As a matter of fact, the survey conducted by *Capital*[17] shows that in 2010 the annual salary range of the CEOs in the Turkish banking sector was between 600,000 TL (400,000 USD) and 2,500,000 TL (1,700,000 USD).

In large companies, top executive remuneration is based on performance. Company size appears to be an important factor in compensation patterns. The salary constitutes the stable part of the remuneration package and variable pay such as incentives and bonuses may increase CEO revenues up to twofold.[18] For example, profit sharing plans, where a certain percentage of the turnover/profit is distributed among the top managers on top of their salary, constitutes the real increase in CEO incomes. To give an example, the Ford Automotive Industry explains its compensation package calculation as follows:[19] Top executives' bonuses are calculated based on company performance and individual performance (i.e., performance-based incentive plan). The base for bonus is revised each year, varying in relation to the size of the top executive's task. During this revision of the bonus base, the prevailing rate in the market for top executive compensation is taken into consideration. Company performance, which is one of the major components of the compensation, is calculated at the end of the year in relation to the fulfillment of the financial and operational (market share, export, international activities, productivity, etc.) objectives. Sustainability and continuous improvement of the performance is emphasized in the formulation of the objectives. Individual performance, on the other hand, focuses on goals related to workforce, clients, processes, technology, and long-term strategies along with the yearly company objectives. Individual performance measurement adopts the principle of long-term sustainable progress.

The highest earning CEOs are found to be those employed by the largest holding companies such as Koç Holding, Doğuş Holding, Sabancı Holding, Borusan Holding, and Eczacıbaşı Holding; the largest banks such as Garanti Bank, Yapı Kredi Bank, and İş Bank, and the largest telecommunication companies such as Turkcell, Vodafone, and Türk Telekom. The following table (Table 7.1), compiled from different company sources by the authors, shows the median of both base salary and the total cash compensation including bonuses for various size companies. The highest compensation can be the double of the median in some sectors and some companies.

Along with salaries and bonuses, CEOs are also offered additional benefits such as life and health insurance, pension plans, various perks (driver, car, rent, some other personal expenses, etc.).

Depending also on the ownership structure and location, there is a wide difference between the compensation levels of managers in different type of companies. For instance, family member managers in a family business group may receive higher salaries and keep their position for decades. However, there is still a difference between the female and male members of the family with respect to attaining the apex of the companies and the respective compensation level.[20] Sons are preferred over daughters to head the family enterprise even if they have a lower education level.

Table 7.1 CEO compensation

| Size of the company (1 = Largest firm) | Base salary (Median) | Total (Median) |
| --- | --- | --- |
| 1 | 48,300,00 TL | 60,600,00 TL |
| 2 | 40,000,00 TL | 59,900,00 TL |
| 3 | 35,400,00 TL | 55,800,00 TL |
| 4 | 32,300,00 TL | 42,000,00 TL |
| 5 | 25,700,00 TL | 30,300,00 TL |
| 6 | 21,400,00 TL | 26,200,00 TL |
| 7 | 18,700,00 TL | 20,600,00 TL |

Source: Compiled from different company databases by the authors in 2015.

The compensation the former receives is much higher and often includes company shares.

The relationship and closeness with the owners are other important determinants of the remuneration. The paternalist culture leads to differential treatments in terms of compensation and distorts performance-reward contingency.[21] The inner circle composed of those who are closer to the superior may receive a preferential treatment and "rewards regardless of their performance."[22] In the same fashion, those who are close to the owners of the company benefit from the same preferential treatment.

Moreover, the geographical position of the company can influence the salary level as well as the extent of the additional benefits. For instance, the compensations seem to be 30 to 35 percent higher in the Istanbul area in comparison with other regions in Turkey.[23]

Another factor influencing the compensation level is the relative scarcity of the type of top executive. During the early years of the industrialization when managers were scarce, the compensation practices were even more generous. For example, during its initial years, the Koç Company used to offer a percentage of the company shares to promising managers, a practice continuing into the1950s.[24] Nowadays, the practice of offering company shares to professional managers is very rare, albeit a few exceptions. This is something mostly practiced by foreign companies. The scarcity of top executives as well as the level of competition in a specific sector raises the salary level in that particular industry.

According to Aycan, the initial salary is agreed upon through negotiations at the beginning, and it is the individual rather than the job that is evaluated, which leads to high salary differences for the same job.[25] She also specifies that salary increases are influenced by inflation rate, performance, and tenure of the individual and his/her favorable relations with influential figures in the company. Similarly, promotion often depends on the level of performance, accomplishment of the trainings, and position tenure.

## Turnover and Succession Planning

According to a poll conducted by Peryön and Towers Watson in 75 companies in 2013, employee turnover is reported to be around 11.5 percent, with an increase of 4 percent over the previous year.[26] The turnover rate seems to be higher for upper echelons. Although the mean tenure of the seems to be rather consistent between 1980s to 2010s with a mean tenure of 6.3 years in 1983,[27] 7.5 years in 1992,[28] and 7 years in 2010,[29] (maximum tenure at the position: 47 years in 1983,[30] 35 in 1992, and 55 in 2010[31]), turnover is more frequent at the CEO level in comparison with lower levels.

A study conducted among the nonfinancial companies quoted in the Istanbul Stock Exchange between 1999 and 2007, reports CEO turnover to be 14 percent; and among all the turnovers, disciplinary turnovers due to poor performance constitute only 14 percent.[32] Disciplinary turnover increases in companies with state ownership.[33] However, state companies are known to be highly political environments where the departures of CEOs as well as their appointments may also be due to political reasons.

Negative corporate performance increases the probability of CEO turnover.[34] Income before tax rather than stock market performance defines corporate performance and influences CEO turnover. A recent study with a sample of 258 companies quoted in Borsa İstanbul found that 57 percent of the companies experienced CEO change between 2005 and 2011.[35] According to this study, around 18 percent of the firms experienced more than one CEO turnover in six years. The overall CEO turnover ranged between 10 and 15 percent, depending on the observation year. Among all the turnovers, disciplinary turnovers were found to be around 7 percent[36] between 2005 and 2011. According to the results of the same study, 64 percent of the CEOs were generally promoted from within in 2005, and 36 percent were hired from other companies. Nonetheless, 60 percent of their successors were mainly transferred from other companies. While around 29 percent of the successors originated from affiliated companies (firms of the same group or central unit of the holding), approximately 31 percent were from unaffiliated companies.[37] Therefore the tradition of promoting the CEO from the company's own talent pool tends to decrease. This can indicate that firms are getting away from inbreeding and becoming more open to other companies and experiences. This seems to be more frequent in the telecommunication sector. For example, the current CEO of Turkcell, Kaan Terzioğlu, and the previous one, Süreyya Ciliv, were transferred from other companies in the technology sector.

Succession planning is very much influenced by the traditions in the case of the family firms where the son is expected to take over the control of the company.[38] As might be expected, the predecessor is usually influential in the selection process. There seems to be a pecking order in the selection of the heir apparent.[39] The oldest son in particular and sons in general are most likely to become the successor in a family enterprise. The daughters are considered as heir apparent usually when there is no male offspring. Even the son-in-law is preferred over the daughter.[40] There were 26 chairwomen and 13 female CEOs in the Borsa İstanbul in 2015, corresponding, respectively, to 6.2 and 3.2 percent of all the listed companies.[41]

Since working at other firms is not perceived in a positive way, the heirs usually start working at the family firm following their graduation from the university.[42] In rare instances, heirs were found to have worked abroad where they go to obtain a higher education degree.[43] One of the rare examples of company policy for extending the experience of the heirs is observed in the Boyner Group: At the beginning of their career, the heirs need to work for at least five years in companies not affiliated with the group.[44]

A queuing system seems to be in place whereby large companies first employ family members for top positions, only filling these positions with professional managers when there is no appropriate candidate in the family.[45] Professionals able to reach top positions generally have long tenures within the company and are perceived as trusted men of the family. In short, the founder or the father dominates the succession process, often with no formal succession planning.[46] Only in a few of the largest family groups such as the Koç Holding are there rules regarding the mandatory retirement age for the CEO; and after the retirement of the incumbent CEO the successor is selected from a large pool of top executives. Although the mandatory retirement age is 60 in the Koç Group, there are also some exceptions.[47] For example, this was extended for Turgay Durak, the previous CEO of the Group, who was 63 when he retired. The Alarko Holding and the Sabancı Holding are also among those implementing the practice of CEO mandatory retirement age and related succession processes.

Succession planning seems to be poor in the case of nonfamily firms as well. There are some trends in selecting the successor. For example, in the banking sector, top executives with a background in the inspection department are favored in succession, but there is usually no predefined successor. In the case of the subsidiaries of the multinationals, the successor CEOs are appointed from the central unit in 40 percent of the cases, and only 30 percent are promoted from within the local subsidiary.[48]

# PART IV
# Conclusions

# CHAPTER 8

# Current and Future Governance Challenges in the Turkish Economy

Corporate governance is defined as the "system of checks and balances, both internal and external to companies, which ensure that companies discharge their accountability to all their stakeholders and act in a socially responsible way in all areas of their business activity."[1] Specific attributes of the business context in Turkey, actually resembling the characteristics of other developing countries, leads to different sets of relevant stakeholders that companies are accountable to. Similarly, a unique perception of corporate social responsibility shapes the relations between society and corporations, influencing the salient corporate governance issues and mechanisms for companies in this business context. Convergence argument in this chapter is based on the relevant stakeholders and the conception of corporate social responsibility, which are delineated by the historical roots, cultural norms, and legal tradition attributable to this specific business context.

## Convergence Toward a Global Model

Apparently there are attempts to converge to shareholder oriented, Anglo American, market-based model by the regulatory authority, the Capital Market Board (CMB) in Turkey. This is rather a convergence in form rather than in function. While the convergence in function implies the fulfillment of the same functions such as ensuring disclosure and accountability of the executives in spite of differing legal frameworks, the convergence in form delineates a growing resemblance in relation to laws and legal institutions.[2] The ongoing attempts to converge laws and regulations regarding governance may also be interpreted as early moves to a "de jure" convergence in Turkey. For example, the requirement of the new Capital Market Law (CML) for the presence of independent directors in the boardroom is a "de jure" convergence. However, in many instances, the directors selected for this position are affiliated in some ways either with the company or with the owners, suggesting that the convergence is not "de facto." There is also a considerable level of decoupling; in other words, despite the claims of conformity and adoption, the new practices are either not implemented or implemented differently.[3]

Convergence toward the shareholder-oriented, Anglo-American model is an outcome of globalization and the neoliberal movement.[4] In Turkey as well, there have been strong external influences in that direction. The economic instability of the 1970s was handled by a "shock therapy,"[5] and, in 1980, export-led industrial policy was adopted with the encouragement of the International Monetary Fund (IMF) and the World Bank.[6] This shift in economic policy toward liberalization and internationalization culminated in the privatization of state economic enterprises and the abandonment of mixed economy and protectionist course of actions. The 1980 military coup eased the transition to liberalization policy strongly encouraged by the international financial institutions such as the IMF and the World Bank. The agreement with the IMF put forward the adoption of good governance principles. In parallel with many countries, Turkey took the Organization for Economic Cooperation and Development (OECD) Corporate Governance Principles (CGP) as a benchmark. The OECD CGP were created by an intergovernmental task force composed of the representatives of the OECD countries, the EU commission, the World Bank, the IMF, and the Bank for International Settlements, as well as the representatives of business and labor who were more in line with the market-based systems due to the fact that most of the OECD countries had market-based systems with supporting regulatory institutions.[7] This OECD benchmark was adopted in Turkey in spite of the lack of supporting regulatory institutions and institutional structure. Eventually, the corporate law and practice converged toward the shareholder value maximization model, which is a form of normative isomorphism. As a matter of fact, countries with weak shareholder protection rights, such as Turkey, are subject to legitimization forces, with markets pushing for the diffusion of codes.[8]

Together with the diffusion of corporate governance codes, harmonization of accounting regulations across the countries, the integration of financial markets (cross-listings in markets with strict regulations, certification impact, institutional investors investing in companies with better compliance) are the other drivers for the adoption of governance principles.[9] Globally integrated product markets and search for low-cost production and capital reinforce the shareholder value maximization model also supported in an ideological and political fashion.[10] Harmonization of the accounting standards in Turkey with the International Financial Standards began in 2005. The new Turkish Commercial Code enacted on January 13, 2011, together with the new CML coming into force on December 30, 2012, have contributed to the strengthening of the financial infrastructure and have generated a significant degree of harmonization with the EU legislation.

Integration with global financial markets is an important motive for countries with a limited investor base and capital. The motivation of Turkey in adopting the OECD governance principles was mainly to attract foreign investors. This has been openly expressed in the foreword of the Turkish CGP by the chairman of the CMB. The aim of gaining and maintaining investor confidence has shifted attention to the principles of transparency, accountability, fairness, and responsibility, and the adoption of CGP. According to the internationally accepted and diffusing model of corporate governance, the main pillars of good governance is composed of the following elements: transparency in relation to accurate and timely disclosure of the activities, fairness in recognizing the moral rights of the relevant parties and respecting the contracts, accountability in terms of establishing the control mechanisms for executive activities to make sure that they correspond to the interest of these relevant parties, and finally responsibility to consider the rights and interests of other stakeholders.[11] Despite the seeming adoption of these pillars in the Turkish context, there are still significant discrepancies in practice.

## Forces Resisting Convergence

The Turkish economy faces many challenges in terms of governance. The characteristics of the business systems make convergence difficult.

Countries vary along their legal framework, corporate ownership structure, and financial system, all leading to different needs in terms of governance.[12]

Legal origin is claimed to be a substantial factor informing governance practices.[13] Civil law and common law countries have different governance traditions. Shareholder right protection is strongest in the common law countries where there are also developed capital markets. Civil law countries are known with their poor investor protection and relatively less developed markets and Turkey is a civil law country as explained in the chapters dedicated to history and legal system. The converging trends for governance are well-suited to common law contexts. Therefore, the civil law context of Turkey presents many peculiarities necessitating a different governance framework to deal with corporate governance challenges proposed by weak protection of private property rights.

As mentioned earlier, Turkey has a relationship-based, insider system of ownership and control structure where the majority of the company shares are held by family, business groups, and the state. This is in contradiction with the outsider system where ownership and control are separated and company shares are thus dispersed among outsider investors.[14] Convergence to the market-based outsider system, which is the normative pressure behind the governance principles, appears to be relatively difficult in the Turkish insider system where (in spite of many improvements), mistreatments of minority shareholders by the blockholders and disclosure problems are still common issues. In civil law countries, the ownership is usually significantly concentrated, and families hold both the ownership and control of the companies. This obviously contradicts with what is observed in market-based systems distinguished by dispersed shareholders and the separation of ownership and management.

A corollary of legal origin is the nature of the financial system. The financial system, which can either be bank- or market-oriented, has also significant impacts on the corporate governance practices. As a consequence of having civil law origin, Turkey has a bank-oriented financial system in which banks, rather than markets, have a determining role in providing funds to companies. This is in contrast to market-oriented systems of the Anglo-American model where the stock market rather than the banks are active in funding the companies with also significant influences on their management.

Similarly, path dependencies stemming from existing structure and rules, variances in property right regulations, and cultural context are among the factors causing divergences in governance regimes.[15] Legislation in relation to corporations such as labor law, commerce law, capital market and financial institutions regulations bring about path dependencies for corporate governance. These laws are also influenced by the path dependencies originating from the dominant structures of the business system. A relevant example might be the case of new Turkish Commerce Law. Several of the items aiming to improve existing governance practices were either restricted to listed companies or removed from the draft at the very last moment due to the pressures of the businesses. There are fundamental complementary parts in each system. For example, independent directors, takeover possibilities, incentive and pay schemes for executives, and disclosure are main components of the Anglo-American governance system.[16] The Turkish system presents quite different characteristics that are hardly compatible with the Anglo-American system. Cross-shareholdings by firms affiliated with the business group, concentrated ownership, high reliance on debt, and absence of takeover market are the main characteristics of the Turkish market.

Property rights regime is another important factor for governance. Allocation and legal enforcement of control rights are largely regulated by the state.[17] Turkey is one of the countries where property rights system is increasingly becoming weak and discretionary. The government has a central role in the allocation and enforcement of property rights where favoritism takes a leading role. Similar to the countries with weak property rights, the Turkish business system is characterized by family ownership and concentrated shareholdings; so, links with the political elites play a critical role in the survival and success of the business. The strong state plays an essential role in the economy as it generates employment for the lower income citizens and provides subsidies and incentives to businesses through frequently changing rules and regulations, which result in discretionary allocations in the economy. This creates a high level of uncertainty in the business environment of the private sector, which is very much dependent on state allocations. Consequently, businesses rely on connections and close interactions with the government for their survival and success. Thus, forming and maintaining good relations with the government become more critical than market-based strategies in the business context. This attribute poses context-specific corporate governance challenges. In addition to leaning on forming and maintaining good relations with the government, family business groups devise different institutional solutions to protect their wealth and to avoid confiscation of their private property. One such institutional solution is the family owned foundations, which are denoted as a corporate governance issue in this context by the OECD, given the assessment that companies pursue noncommercial activities in the form of philanthropic activities of the controlling families by diverting profits to family owned foundations. Additionally, corporate governance laws and their enforcement are under the influence of this discriminatory and discretionary nature of the state-based allocations and enforcement of control rights. Although laws and regulations with respect to corporate governance have been enacted, enforcement of these laws and regulations still remains weak.

Finally, Licht[18] identifies culture as one of the main path dependencies and barriers against convergence. Indeed, the cultural aspects of Turkish context with its emphasis on patriarchy and paternalism, high scores on power distance, low tolerance for ambiguity, and collectivistic understanding with a weaker focus on performance, present a totally different atmosphere in comparison with the cultural milieu of the Anglo-American context. Governance principles effectively in force are not able to address the relevant corporate governance issues of the business context in Turkey. Convergence is in form rather than in substance, and this is so mainly for legitimization purposes, as is the case in other civil law countries.

## Triggers for Change?

There are counter forces regarding the triggers for change in Turkish corporate governance originating from different layers as identified by Clarke,[19] who points out to the multilayered nature of governance. The highest level is the global level where the identification of global problems for the global agenda takes place and influence the flow of investment at a global scale by multinationals. The next level is the institutional level where institutions such as the OECD and governments perceive the problems in relation to governance and propose solutions. The nongovernmental organizations (NGOs) and corporations form the organizational level and provide responses to the issues of governance. Finally, perceptions on governance constitute the managerial level.

When the particularities of the Turkish context are taken into account, it is observed that the global and institutional level influences have always been powerful in shaping the governance framework. Historically, during the Ottoman era, Western governments and corporations have been the leading forces to introduce changes into the governance framework. Similarly, in recent times, following the globalization, the IMF and other international financial institutions insisted for a change in the corporate governance system in Turkey. The conditions for the stabilization package relating to the stand-by credit from the IMF in 2001 dictated that Turkey introduces good governance both to private and public sectors. The CMB introduced the CGP in 2003 based on the OECD principles and revised them in 2005, following the revision of the OECD principles in 2004. Harmonization of accounting rules and diffusion of governance principles across countries, stock exchanges, professional associations of managers and different trades appear as the drivers of the convergence toward shareholder-oriented Anglo-American, market-based model of governance. There are, however, conflicting signals on the part of the government in Turkey. While various initiatives are taken to adapt the related legal framework to the shareholder-oriented, Anglo-American market-based model (e.g., the CML), there are also increasing attempts to erode the fundamental pillars of governance such as property rights and the rule of law. Existing triggers of change at the institutional level as identified by Clarke seem rather conflictual when we compare international forces and government actions. While the former promotes convergence to the Anglo-American model, the latter adopts a discretionary and discriminatory process with changing rules from one case to another leading to an idiosyncratic or degenerated model. Discriminatory processes applied to Doğan Holding, Koç Holding, among others, are clear examples of this inconsistent grounds for governance. This state-induced uncertainty makes it difficult to exactly predict the prospective orientation of governance in Turkey.

Similarly, there are countervailing triggers of change both at the organizational level and managerial level. At the organizational level, the

NGOs and corporations have diverging stances. Organizations such as the Turkish Corporate Governance Association or the Turkish Industrialist and Businessmen Association favor the convergence to ease integration with the global markets. As representatives of the business sector, these NGOs work closely with international organizations and the government in setting the CGP and their dissemination. On the other hand, corporations report difficulties in applying proposed "good governance principles" derived from the OECD governance principles. Analyses of disclosures relating to corporate governance practices reveal compliance in form rather than compliance in substance of the principles. Compliance reports include explanations on reasons of noncompliance as well as declarations on compliance for practices that actually represent noncompliance, reflecting a misconception about the substance of the principles. Difficulties in applying the principles and misconceptions about their substance seem to be the underlying factors for divergence. Moreover, the fact that privately held companies are not required to adopt these principles also acts as a factor for divergence in this context, where only a limited number of companies are listed in stock exchange. Some of the CGP have become compulsory legal requirements in the recent overhaul of the Turkish Commercial Code and entered the realm of privately held companies. However, differing perceptions about corporate governance have blocked some of these principles in entering the laws, which indicates the presence of differing views at the managerial level as well. One such area of divergent opinions at the managerial level is transparency and disclosure.

As a conclusion, we can assert that there are countervailing triggers for change at different levels, with important forces leading to divergence in terms of governance model. However, this divergence is far from creating a genuine model. Global and institutional level influences seem to be critical in shaping the corporate governance environment in the business context of Turkey. While the government is adopting CGP in a way to converge with the market-oriented Anglo-American model, its actions are leading to discretionary and discriminatory practices in governance, which ultimately creates a rather inconsistent governance atmosphere where it is difficult to predict future orientations. Additionally, weaknesses in the governance environment, such as rule of law, protection of private property rights, regulatory quality, and voice and accountability, have detrimental impacts on the corporate governance environment. In such a context, corporations develop firm-level corporate governance mechanisms in order to overcome the weaknesses in the governance environment. A genuine model needs to be developed, which is more inclusive of these divergent firm-level practices of the corporations emerging in response to the specific characteristics of the context. Increasing accountability at the firm level and ensuring democratic forms of governance at the institutional level can support this genuine model, while converging with the basic principles of good governance such as transparency, accountability, fairness, and responsibility.

# Abbreviations

| | |
|---|---|
| AKP | Adalet ve Kalkınma Partisi—Justice and Development Party |
| BBVA | Banco Bilbao Vizcaya Argentaria |
| BILTEN | Information Technologies and Electronics Institute |
| BIST | Borsa Istanbul |
| BSEC | Organization of the Black Sea Economic Cooperation |
| CEO | Chief Executive Officer |
| CFO | Chief Financial Officer |
| CGP | Corporate Governance Principles |
| CHP | Cumhuriyet Halk Partisi—Republican People's Party |
| CMB | Capital Market Board |
| CML | Capital Market Law |
| D-8 | Developing 8 |
| DDY | Devlet Demir Yolları—State Railways |
| EÜAŞ | Elektrik Üretim A.Ş.—Electricity Production Inc. |
| EU | European Union |
| ECO | Economic Cooperation Organization |
| EFTA | European Free Trade Association |
| FBGs | Family Business Groups |
| GCI | Global Competitiveness Index |
| GDP | Gross Domestic Product |
| HR | Human Resources |
| IMF | International Monetary Fund |
| IPO | Initial Public Offerings |
| ISA | International Standards on Auditing |
| ISE | Istanbul Stock Exchange |
| KAP | Kamuyu Aydınlatma Platformu—Public Disclosure Platform |
| MENA | Middle East and North Africa |
| MKK | Merkezi Kayıt Kuruluşu—Central Securities Depository Institution |
| MÜSİAD | Müstakil Sanayici ve İşadamları Derneği—The Association of Independent Industrialists and Business people |
| OECD | Organization for Economic Cooperation and Development |
| OIC | Organization for Islamic Cooperation |
| OYAK | Ordu Yardımlaşma Kurumu—Turkish Armed Forces Assistance Fund |

| | |
|---|---|
| PTT | Posta ve Telgraf Teşkilatı—The Postal and Telegraph Agency |
| SMEs | Small- and Medium-Sized Enterprises |
| SPA | Share Purchase Agreement |
| TCA | Turkish Contractors Associations |
| TCC | Turkish Commercial Code |
| TETAŞ | Türkiye Elektrik Ticaret ve Taahhüt Şirketi—Turkish Electricity Trade and Contracting Corporation |
| TL | Turkish Lira |
| TUSKON | Türkiye İşadamları ve Sanayiciler Konfederasyonu—The Confederation of Turkish Businesspeople and Industrialists |
| TÜPRAŞ | Türkiye Petrol Rafinerileri Anonim Şirketi Turkish Petroleum Refineries Corporation |
| TÜSİAD | Türk Sanayicileri ve İşadamları Derneği—Turkish Association of Industrialists and Businessmen |
| TÜYİD | Türkiye Yatırımcı İlişkileri Derneği—Turkish Investor Relations Society |
| WEF | World Economic Forum |

# Notes

## Chapter 1

1. TÜİK (2015a).
2. IMF (2016).
3. World Bank (2014c, pp. 4–23).
4. World Bank (2014c).
5. World Bank (2016a).
6. World Bank (2014c).
7. Öniş and Şenses (2007).
8. Manktelow (2014).
9. World Bank (2014c).
10. Hoskisson et al. (2013).
11. World Bank (2014c).
12. European Commission (2014).
13. Sustainable Governance Indicators (2015).
14. Acemoglu and Robinson (2013).
15. World Bank (2014c).
16. La Porta, Lopez-de-Silanes, and Shleifer (2008).
17. World Bank (2014c, a).
18. Öniş and Şenses (2007).
19. Erçek and Günçavdı (2016).
20. Karabag and Berggren (2014).
21. Keyman and Koyuncu (2005).
22. Manktelow (2014).
23. Pamuk (2014).
24. Öniş and Şenses (2007).
25. Eğilmez (2015).
26. TÜİK (2015b).
27. Undersecretariat of Treasury (2015).
28. Pamuk (2014).
29. Pamuk (2014).
30. Öniş and Şenses (2007).
31. Undersecretariat of Treasury (2015).
32. Peker and Candemir (2015).
33. World Bank (2013).
34. TÜİK (2015b).

35. Ertuna, Ercan, and Akgiray (2003).
36. World Bank (2014d).
37. World Bank (2014d).
38. The Economist (2014b).
39. Marois (2012).
40. European Commission (2014).
41. Gönenç et al. (2014).
42. Gönenç et al. (2014).
43. Hürriyet Gazetesi (2015).
44. İstanbul Chamber of Industry (2010).
45. Borsa İstanbul (2014b).
46. Ertuna, Ercan, and Akgiray (2003).
47. Yamak and Ertuna (2012).
48. Borsa İstanbul (2014b).
49. World Bank (2016b).
50. World Bank (2014a).
51. World Bank (2014a).
52. World Economic Forum (2014).
53. World Economic Forum (2014).
54. World Economic Forum (2014).
55. UNDP (2014).
56. Ülengin et al. (2011).
57. Öniş and Şenses (2007).
58. Manktelow (2014).
59. Pamuk (2014).
60. World Bank (2016b).
61. TÜİK (2014).
62. TÜİK (2014).
63. TÜİK (2014).
64. Gros and Selçuki (2013).
65. World Trade Organization (2014).
66. World Bank (2016b).
67. World Bank (2016b).
68. World Bank (2016b).
69. World Trade Organization (2014).
70. Cebeci and Fernandes (2015).
71. Cebeci and Fernandes (2015).
72. World Bank (2016b).
73. Ekonomi Bakanlığı (2012).
74. World Bank (2014c).
75. Ekonomi Bakanlığı (2015a).

76. World Bank (2014b).
77. World Bank (2016b).
78. The Economist (2014a).
79. The Economist (2014a).
80. Ekonomi Bakanlığı (2015b).
81. World Bank (2016b).

# Chapter 2

1. United Nations Refugee Agency (2016).
2. U.S. Department of State Bureau of Democracy, Human Rights and Labor (2015).
3. U.S. Department of State Bureau of Democracy, Human Rights and Labor (2015).
4. Esmer (2012).
5. Esmer (2012).
6. Berkes (1978).
7. Ergur, Yamak, and Özbilgin (2015, pp. 112).
8. Yamak and Ertuna (2012, pp. 470–98).
9. Christensen (2007, pp. 179–99).
10. Buğra (1994).
11. Çiftçi (2011, pp. 623–44).
12. Timur (1989).
13. Yamak (2006, pp. 206–12).
14. Tezel (2002, pp. 5–149).
15. Şanda (1978).
16. Akyıldız (2001, pp. 19–45).
17. Akyıldız (2001, pp. 19–45).
18. İnalcık (1998).
19. İnalcık (1998).
20. Akyıldız (2001, pp. 20–45).
21. Toprak (1995a).
22. Akyıldız (2001, p. 48).
23. Akyıldız (2001, p. 49).
24. Toprak (1995b).
25. Şanda (1978).
26. Akyıldız (2001, p. 21).
27. Esirgen (2011, pp. 31–48).
28. Akyıldız (2001, pp. 20–29).
29. Poroy (1988).
30. Toprak (1995a).

31. Akyıldız (2001, pp. 23–24).
32. Akyıldız (2001).
33. Şanda (1978).
34. Toprak (1995b).
35. Akyıldız (2001, pp. 20–45).
36. Clark (1969).
37. Yamak (2006, pp. 206–12).
38. Buğra (1994, pp. 38–39).
39. Şaylan (1974).
40. Yamak (2006, pp. 206–12).
41. Yamak (2006, pp. 206–12).
42. Roos and Roos (1971).
43. Yamak (2006, pp. 206–12).
44. Yamak (2006, pp. 206–12).
45. Yamak (2006, p. 209).
46. Roos and Roos (1971).
47. Yamak (2006, pp. 206–12).
48. Yamak (2006, p. 212).
49. Yamak (2006, pp. 206–12).
50. Boratav, Türel, and Yeldan (1996, pp. 373–93).
51. Yamak and Üsdiken (2006, pp. 177–94).
52. Yamak et al. (2015, pp. 1474–97).
53. İlkin (1971, pp. 199–233).
54. İlkin (1971, pp. 199–233).
55. İlkin (1971, pp. 199–233).
56. Üsdiken (2008, pp. 5–21).
57. Bilgişin (1936).
58. Kuyucak (1939).
59. Tezel (2002, pp. 5–149).
60. Nilsson (2007, pp. 195–236).
61. Atakan, Özsoy, and Oba (2008, pp. 201–16).
62. Nilsson (2007, pp. 195–236).
63. Capital Market Board (2015).
64. Marois (2012).
65. Marois (2012).
66. Marois (2012).
67. Marois (2012).
68. World Bank (2014c, p. 4).
69. Altay and Amasya (2007).
70. Dal and Çalış (2013, pp. 87–106).
71. Yamak and Ertuna (2012, pp. 470–98).

72. World Economic Forum (2014).
73. World Economic Forum (2014).
74. OECD (2014).
75. OECD (2014).
76. OECD (2014).
77. Transparency International (2015).
78. Transparency International (2015).
79. Marois (2012, p. 5).
80. Marois (2012).
81. World Bank (2014c).
82. World Bank (2014c).
83. Pesqueux, Yamak, and Süer (2004).
84. Özcan and Çokgezen (2003, pp. 2061–84).
85. Özcan and Çokgezen (2003, p. 2061).
86. The Economist (2012).
87. Herbert Smith Freehills Dispute Resolution (2015).
88. Herbert Smith Freehills Dispute Resolution (2015).
89. KAP (2015c).
90. Nebil (2015).
91. Nebil (2015).

# Chapter 3

1. La Porta, Lopez-de-Silanes, and Shleifer (2008).
2. La Porta, Lopez-de-Silanes, and Shleifer (2008).
3. Küçükgüngör (2014).
4. Atakan, Özsoy, and Oba (2008).
5. Sermaye Piyasası Kurulu (2014).
6. OECD (2013).
7. OECD (2013).
8. Sermaye Piyasası Kurulu (2014).
9. Nilsson (2007).
10. Altay and Amasya (2007).
11. OECD (2013).
12. Düzel (2012).
13. Düzel (2012).
14. Atakan, Özsoy, and Oba (2008).
15. Altay and Amasya (2007).
16. Sonmez (2014).
17. Kort (2008).
18. Resmi Gazete (2012).

19. Türk Ticaret Kanunu (2011).
20. Atakan, Özsoy, and Oba (2008).
21. IIF EAG (2005).
22. Sermaye Piyasası Kurulu (2014).
23. Yurtoğlu (2000).
24. Nilsson (2007).
25. IIF EAG (2005).
26. Nilsson (2007).
27. Orbay and Yurtoğlu (2006).
28. IIF EAG (2005).
29. La Porta, Lopez-de-Silanes, Shleifer, and Vishny (1998).
30. *Worldwide Governance Indicators* (2014).
31. *Worldwide Governance Indicators* (2014).
32. *Worldwide Governance Indicators* (2014).
33. Gönenç et al. (2014).
34. Gönenç et al. (2014).
35. Gönenç et al. (2014).
36. World Economic Forum (2014).
37. World Bank (2014).
38. Gönenç et al. (2014).
39. World Bank (2014a).
40. Ministry of Labour and Social Security (2014).
41. World Bank (2014c).
42. Ozkan, Balsari, and Varan (2014).
43. Sustainable Governance Indicators (2015).
44. Tuan and Arıoğlu (2014).
45. OECD (2014).
46. OECD (2014).
47. Public Oversight, Accounting and Auditing Standards Authority (2015).
48. OECD (2013).
49. Yurtoğlu (2000).
50. OECD (2013).
51. Ertuna and Tükel (2013).

# Chapter 4

1. Kabasakal and Bodur (2007, p. 844).
2. Aycan (2001, pp. 1–26).
3. Aycan (2006b, pp. 160–80).
4. Aycan (2006a, pp. 455–66).
5. Aycan (2006b, pp. 160–80).

6. Aycan (2006a, pp. 455–66).
7. Aycan (2006b, pp. 160–80).
8. Hofstede (1980); Hofstede (2001); Kabasakal and Bodur (2007, pp. 835–74).
9. Oba, Özsoy, and Atakan (2010, pp. 603–16).
10. Kabasakal and Bodur (2007, pp. 835–74).
11. Trompenaars and Hampden-Turner (1998); Schwartz (1994).
12. World Economic Forum (2014).
13. Aksu and Kosedag (2006, pp. 277–96).
14. Kabasakal and Bodur (2007, p. 842).
15. Kabasakal and Bodur (2007, pp. 835–74).
16. Esmer (2012).
17. Aycan et al. (2000, pp. 192–220).
18. Ergüder, Esmer, and Kalaycıoğlu (1991).
19. Aygün, Arslan, and Güney (2008, pp. 205–23).
20. Aslan (2001, pp. 321–339).
21. Askun, Oz, and Olcay (2010, pp. 103–14).
22. Çatalbaş (2007, pp. 19–35).
23. Öncü (2013, pp. 125–36).
24. Öncü (2013, pp. 125–36).
25. Öncü (2013, pp. 125–36).
26. Çatalbaş (2007, pp. 19–35).
27. Öncü (2013, pp. 125–36).
28. Christensen (2007, pp. 179–99).
29. Christensen (2007, pp. 179–99).
30. Çatalbaş (2007, pp. 19–35).
31. Reporters Without Borders (2016).
32. Reporters Without Borders (2016).
33. The Economist (2013).
34. Rethink Institute (2014, p. 1).
35. Rethink Institute (2014, p. 1).
36. Çatalbaş (2007, pp. 19–35).
37. Christensen (2007, pp. 179–99).
38. Öncü (2013, p. 125).
39. Freedom House (2015).
40. Freedom House (2015).
41. Freedom House (2015).
42. Freedom House (2015).
43. Genckaya, Togan, and Schulz (2015).
44. Yeginsu (2015).
45. Freedom House (2015).

46. Freedom House (2014a).

47. Yanardağoğlu (2013, pp. 87–102).

48. Christensen (2007, p. 196).

49. Yeginsu (2015).

50. PEN International (2016).

51. Freedom House (2014b).

52. Freedom House (2014b).

53. Freedom House (2014b).

54. TÜSİAD (2014).

55. Ertürk (2003, pp. 185–204).

56. Uğur and Ararat (2006, pp. 325–48).

57. OECD (2013).

58. Yamak and Ertuna (2012, pp. 470–98).

59. Kort (2008, pp. 379–421).

60. OECD (2013).

61. OECD (2006).

62. Arçelik (2013).

63. Oba, Özsoy, and Atakan (2010, pp. 603–16).

64. Ertuna and Tükel (2007).

65. Agca and Önder (2007, pp. 241–251).

66. Agca and Önder (2007, pp. 241–251).

67. Uğur and Ararat (2006, pp. 325–48).

68. KAP (2015a).

69. Borsa İstanbul (2014a).

70. OECD (2013).

71. Atakan, Özsoy, and Oba (2008, pp. 201–16).

72. Borsa İstanbul (2015a).

73. Atakan, Özsoy, and Oba (2008, pp. 201–16).

74. Atakan, Özsoy, and Oba (2008, pp. 201–16).

# Chapter 5

1. La Porta, Lopez-de-Silanes, and Shleifer (1999, pp. 471–517).

2. Leuz, Lins, and Warnock (2009, pp. 3245–85).

3. La Porta, Lopez-de-Silanes, and Shleifer (2008, pp. 285–332).

4. European Commission (2014).

5. La Porta, Lopez-de-Silanes, and Shleifer (1999, pp. 471–517).

6. Claessens, Djankov, and Lang (2000, pp. 81–112).

7. Mandacı and Gumus (2010, pp. 57–66).

8. Demirağ and Serter (2003, pp. 40–51).

9. Orbay and Yurtoğlu (2006, pp. 349–63).

10. Whitley (1994, pp. 153–82).

11. Yurtoğlu (2000, pp. 193–222).

12. Yurtoğlu (2000, pp. 193–222).

13. Orbay and Yurtoğlu (2006, pp. 349–63).

14. Gugler, Mueller, and Yurtoğlu (2008, pp. 688–705).

15. Demirağ and Serter (2003, pp. 40–51).

16. Demirağ and Serter (2003, pp. 40–51).

17. La Porta et al. (2002, pp. 1147–70).

18. Yamak and Ertuna (2012, pp. 470–98).

19. TÜYİD and MKK (2015).

20. Yamak and Ertuna (2012, pp. 470–98).

21. Yamak and Ertuna (2012, pp. 470–98).

22. Colpan (2012).

23. Whitley (1994, pp. 153–82).

24. Guillen (2001).

25. Buğra (1994).

26. Karabag and Berggren (2014, pp. 2212–23).

27. Buğra (1994).

28. Selekler-Gökşen and Üsdiken (2001, pp. 325–40).

29. Colpan and Jones (2015).

30. Erçek and Günçavdı (2016, pp. 89–110).

31. Buğra (1994).

32. Buğra (1994).

33. Colpan and Jones (2015).

34. Üsdiken (2008, pp. 5–21).

35. Sabancı (1985).

36. Üsdiken (2008, pp. 5–21).

37. Colpan (2012).

38. The Economist (2014b).

39. Yamak and Ertuna (2010).

40. Gürsoy and Aydoğan (2002, pp. 6–25).

41. Yamak and Ertuna (2010).

42. Yurtoğlu (2003, pp. 72–86).

43. Ararat and Yurtoğlu (2006, pp. 5–44).

44. Yurtoğlu (2000, pp. 193–222).

45. Üsdiken (2008, pp. 5–21).

46. Yildirim-Öktem and Üsdiken (2007).

47. Yurtoğlu (2003, pp. 72–86).

48. Selekler-Gökşen and Üsdiken (2001, pp. 325–40).

49. Selekler-Göksen and Karatas (2008, pp. 132–47).

50. Üsdiken and Yildirim-Öktem (2008, pp. 43–71).

51. Selekler-Gökşen and Üsdiken (2001, pp. 325–40).

52. Yurtoğlu (2000, pp. 193–222).

53. Yamak, Ertuna, and Bolak (2006, pp. 85–105).

54. Yamak, Ertuna, and Bolak (2006, pp. 85–105).

55. Selekler-Gökşen and Karatas (2008, pp. 132–47).

56. Yurtoğlu (2000, pp. 193–222).

57. Yamak and Ertuna (2010).

58. Colpan (2012).

59. Üsdiken (2008, pp. 5–21).

60. Oba, Tigrel, and Sener (2014, pp. 382–94).

61. Buğra (1994).

62. Buğra (1994).

63. Ertuna (2013, pp. 438–54).

64. OECD (2006).

65. The Economist (2014b).

66. Erçek and Günçavdı (2016, pp. 89–110).

67. Elginkan Holding (2004).

68. Koç (1983).

69. Koç (1991).

70. Özer (2014, pp. 351–77).

71. Özer (2014, pp. 351–77).

72. İş Bankası (2015).

73. Borsa İstanbul (2015b).

74. OYAK (1961).

75. OYAK (2014).

76. Oktar (2007).

77. Capital Dergisi (2002).

78. OYAK (2014).

79. Capital Dergisi (2002).

80. İstanbul Chamber of Industry (2015).

81. OYAK (2014).

82. Colpan (2012).

83. Privatization Administration (2016).

84. Privatization Administration (2016).

85. İstanbul Chamber of Industry (2014).

86. Colpan (2012).

87. EÜAŞ (2010).

88. Yamak and Ertuna (2010).

89. Privatization Administration (2016).

90. Nilsson (2007, pp. 195–236).

91. İş Bankası (2014).

92. Yurtoğlu (2000, pp. 193–222).

93. Nilsson (2007, pp. 195–236).
94. OECD (2013).
95. Ertuna and Tükel (2013, pp. 31–57).
96. OECD (2013).
97. Leuz, Lins, and Warnock (2009, pp. 3245–85).
98. Yamak and Ertuna (2010).
99. Ertuna and Yamak (2011, pp. 117–128).
100. Ertuna and Tükel (2013, pp. 31–57).
101. Yamak et al. (2015, pp. 263–81).
102. KAP (2015d).
103. Burgan Bank (2015).
104. Yurtoğlu (2000, pp. 193–222).
105. Ertuna and Tükel (2013, pp. 31–57).
106. OECD (2013).
107. Ararat and Muzaffer (2012).

# Chapter 6

1. Yurtoğlu (2003, pp. 72–86).
2. Aslantaş and Fındıklı (2010, pp. 258–75).
3. Oba, Tigrel, and Sener (2014, pp. 382–94).
4. Selekler-Göksen and Yildirim-Öktem (2009, pp. 193–213).
5. Yıldırım-Öktem and Üsdiken (2010, pp. 115–30).
6. Ertuna and Yamak (2011, pp. 117–28).
7. KAP (2015b).
8. İstanbul Chamber of Industry (2015).
9. Fortune (2016).
10. TÜPRAŞ (2016).
11. TCDD (2014).
12. TCDD (2016).
13. TETAŞ (2016).
14. PTT (2016).
15. Aslantaş and Fındıklı (2010, pp. 258–75).
16. Oba, Tigrel, and Sener (2014, pp. 382–94).
17. Aslantaş and Fındıklı (2010, pp. 258–75).
18. OYAK (2015).
19. OYAK (2016).
20. Elginkan Holding (2004).
21. Herdem (2013).
22. Selekler-Gökşen and Üsdiken (2001, pp. 325–40).
23. Selekler-Gökşen and Karatas (2008, pp. 132–47).
24. Selekler-Göksen and Yildirim-Öktem (2009, pp. 193–213).

25. Yildirim-Öktem and Üsdiken (2007).
26. Selekler-Gökşen and Karatas (2008, pp. 132–47).
27. Ataay (2016a, pp. 106–16).
28. Üsdiken and Yildirim-Öktem (2008, pp. 43–71).
29. Ataay (2016a, pp. 106–16).
30. Ataay (2016a, pp. 106–16).
31. Ataay (2016a, pp. 106–16).
32. Üsdiken and Yildirim-Öktem (2008, pp. 43–71).
33. Ararat, Orbay, and Yurtoğlu (2010).
34. Üsdiken and Yildirim-Öktem (2008, pp. 43–71).
35. Boston Consulting Group (2006).
36. Selekler-Gökşen and Üsdiken (2001, pp. 325–40); Selekler-Gökşen and Karatas (2008, pp. 132–47).
37. Kula (2005, pp. 265–76).
38. Üsdiken and Yildirim-Öktem (2008, pp. 43–71).
39. Üsdiken and Yildirim-Öktem (2008, pp. 43–71).
40. Üsdiken and Yildirim-Öktem (2008, pp. 43–71).
41. Üsdiken and Yildirim-Öktem (2008, pp. 43–71).
42. Ararat, Orbay, and Yurtoğlu (2010).
43. Üsdiken and Yildirim-Öktem (2008, pp. 43–71).
44. De Jonghe, Disli, and Schoors (2012, pp. 51–80).
45. OECD (2013).
46. OECD (2013, p. 80).
47. OECD (2013).
48. Oba, Tigrel, and Sener (2014, pp. 382–94).
49. Grosvold (2011, pp. 531–55).
50. Ararat, Orbay, and Yurtoğlu (2010).
51. Ararat, Alkan, and Aytekin (2015).
52. Yamak et al. (2015, pp. 263–81).
53. Çiftçi (2016).
54. KAP (2016a).
55. KAP (2016b).
56. Yurtoğlu (2000, pp. 193–222).
57. Yamak, Ertuna, and Bolak (2006, pp. 85–105).
58. Yamak and Ergur (2014).
59. Durukan, Ozkan, and Dalkilic (2012, pp. 421–42).
60. Kula (2005, pp. 265–76).
61. Ararat, Alkan, and Aytekin (2015).
62. Sabancı Group (2016).
63. Forbes (2016).
64. Elginkan Holding (2016).
65. Ararat, Alkan, and Aytekin (2015).

66. OVM Petrol Ofisi (2016).
67. Fortune (2016).
68. World Economic Forum (2014).
69. Kort (2008, pp. 379–421).
70. Oba, Özsoy, and Atakan (2010, pp. 603–16).
71. Oba, Özsoy, and Atakan (2010, pp. 603–16).
72. Oba, Özsoy, and Atakan (2010, p. 610).
73. Oba, Özsoy, and Atakan (2010, pp. 603–16).

# Chapter 7

1. Bilgincan (2015).
2. Yamak, Ertuna, and Bolak (2006, pp. 85–105).
3. Erçek (2006, pp. 648–72).
4. Aycan (2008, pp. 359–71).
5. Kalder (2015).
6. Koç Holding (2015a).
7. Koç Holding (2015b).
8. Doğuş Holding (2015).
9. Aycan (2008, pp. 359–71).
10. Sermaye Piyasası Kurulu (2015).
11. Ford Otosan (2015).
12. Oba, Tigrel, and Sener (2014, pp. 382–94).
13. Ertuna and Tükel (2007).
14. OECD (2006).
15. Bayiksel (2009).
16. Bayiksel (2009).
17. Gözütok (2010).
18. Bayiksel (2009).
19. Ford Otosan (2015).
20. Yamak et al. (2016, pp. 125–46).
21. Aycan (2006a, pp. 455–66).
22. Aycan (2006b, pp. 160–80).
23. Aksakal (2008).
24. Yamak (2006, pp. 206–14).
25. Aycan (2008, pp. 359–71).
26. Peryön and Towers Watson (2014).
27. Yamak (1996, pp. 125–130).
28. Yamak (1996, pp. 125–130).
29. Oba, Tigrel, and Sener (2014, pp. 382–94).
30. Yamak (1996, pp. 125–130).
31. Oba, Tigrel, and Sener (2014, pp. 382–94).

32. Durukan, Ozkan, and Dalkılıç (2012, pp. 421–42).
33. Durukan, Ozkan, and Dalkılıç (2012, pp. 421–42).
34. Durukan, Ozkan, and Dalkılıç (2012, pp. 421–42).
35. Ataay (2016b).
36. Ataay (2016b).
37. Ataay (2016b).
38. Tatoglu, Kula, and Glaister (2008, pp. 155–80).
39. Yamak et al. (2016, pp. 125–46).
40. Yamak et al. (2016).
41. Ararat, Alkan, and Aytekin (2015).
42. Tatoglu, Kula, and Glaister (2008, pp. 155–80).
43. Yamak and Ergur (2014).
44. Family Business Advisors (2007).
45. Özbilgin (2011, pp. 275–89).
46. Tatoglu, Kula, and Glaister (2008, pp. 155–80).
47. Güler (2015).
48. Tatoglu, Kula, and Glaister (2008, pp. 155–80).

# Chapter 8

1. Solomon and Solomon (2004, p. 14).
2. Gilson (2004, pp. 128–58).
3. Yoshikawa and Rasheed (2009, pp. 388–404).
4. Marois (2012).
5. Boratav, Turel, and Yeldan (1996, pp. 373–93).
6. Yamak and Üsdiken (2006, pp. 177–94).
7. Davies and Schlitzer (2008, pp. 532–44).
8. Aguilera and Cuervo-Cazurra (2004, pp. 415–43).
9. Yoshikawa and Rasheed (2009, pp. 388–404).
10. Yoshikawa and Rasheed (2009, pp. 388–404).
11. West (2009, pp. 107–19).
12. Davies and Schlitzer (2008, pp. 532–544).
13. La Porta, Lopez-de-Silanez, and Shleifer (1999, pp. 471–517).
14. Bhasa (2004, pp. 5–17).
15. Yoshikawa and Rasheed (2009, pp. 388–404).
16. Aguilera et al. (2008, pp. 475–92).
17. Milhaupt (2004, pp. 21–51).
18. Licht (2000).
19. Clarke (2004).

# References

Acemoglu, D., and J.A. Robinson. 2013. *Why Nations Fail: The Origins of Power, Prosperity and Poverty*. London: Profile Books Ltd.

Agca, A., and Ş. Önder. 2007. "Voluntary Disclosure in Turkey: A Study on Firms Listed in Istanbul Stock Exchange." *Problems and Perspectives in Management* 5, no. 3, pp. 241–51.

Aguilera, R.V., and A. Cuervo-Cazurra. 2004. "Codes of Good Governance Worldwide: What Is the Trigger?" *Organization Studies* 25, no. 3, pp. 415–43.

Aguilera, R.V., I. Filatotchev, H. Gospel, and G. Jackson. 2008. "An Organizational Approach to Comparative Corporate Governance: Costs, Contingencies, and Complementarities." *Organization Science* 19, no. 3, pp. 475–92.

Aksakal, A.T. 2008. "İstanbul'la Ücret Makası Açılıyor mu?" *Capital*, Retrieved from www.capital.com.tr/yonetim/insan-kaynaklari/istanbul'la-ucret-makasi-aciliyor-mu-haberdetay-4934 (accessed January 25, 2016).

Aksu, M., and A. Kosedag. 2006. "Transparency and Disclosure Scores and Their Determinants in The Istanbul Stock Exchange." *Corporate Governance: An International Review* 14, no. 4, pp. 277–96.

Akyıldız, A. 2001. *Osmanlı Dönemi Tahvil ve Hisse Senetleri*. Istanbul: Tarih Vakfı.

Altay, A.S., and S. Amasya. 2007. *Draft of The New Code of Commerce: New Challenges for Turkish Commercial Law*. Istanbul, https://tr.scribd.com/document/3040382/Draft-of-the-New-Turkish-Code-of-Commerce-New-Challenges-for-Turkish-Commercial-Law

Ararat, M., S. Alkan, and B. Aytekin. 2015. *Women on Board Turkey (3rd Annual Report: Independent Women Directors Project)*. Retrieved from https://research.sabanciuniv.edu/29132/1/Women_on_board_Turkey_2015_3rd_Annual_Report.pdf (accessed January 18, 2016).

Ararat, M., and M. Eroglu. 2012. "Istanbul Stock Exchange Moves First on Mandatory Electronic Voting at General Meetings of Shareholders." *SSRN Electronic Journal*. Retrieved from http://papers.ssrn.com/sol3/papers.cfm?abstract_id=2172964 (accessed March 1, 2014).

Ararat, M., H. Orbay, and B. Yurtoğlu. 2010. "The Effects of Board Independence in Controlled Firms: Evidence From Turkey." *SSRN Electronic Journal*. doi: 10.2139/ssrn.1663403 (accessed January 20, 2016).

Ararat, M., and B. Yurtoğlu. 2006. "Yönetişim ve Küresel Rekabet." *Yönetim Araştırmaları Dergisi* 6, nos. 1–2, pp. 5–44.

Arçelik. 2013. "Kurumsal Yönetim Ilkeleri Uyum Raporu." Retrieved from www.arcelikas.com/UserFiles/file/KUY13.pdf (accessed January 26, 2016).

Askun, D., E.U. Oz, and O.B. Askun. 2010. "Understanding Managerial Work Values in Turkey." *Journal of Business Ethics* 93, no. 1, pp. 103–14.

Aslan, M. 2001. "The Work Ethic Values of Protestant British, Catholic Irish and Muslim Turkish Managers." *Journal of Business Ethics* 31, no. 4, pp. 321–39.

Aslantaş, C.C., and M.A. Fındıklı. 2010. "IMKB-50'de Yer Alan Sirketlerin Yönetim Kurulu Yapılanmaları." *İstanbul Universitesi Isletme Fakültesi Dergisi* 39, no. 2, pp. 258–75.

Ataay, A. 2016a. "Roles of Interlocking Directorates in an Emerging Country: Control and Coordination in Family Business Groups." *Journal of Business and Management* 4, no. 2, pp. 106–16.

Ataay, A. 2016b. "Genel Müdür Değişimleri: Ne Sıklıkta Değişiyorlar ve Halefleri Kimler?" *Yonetim Arastirmalari Dergisi.*

Atakan, S., Z. Özsoy, and B. Oba. 2008. "Implementation of Good Corporate Governance in Turkey: The Case of Dogan Yayın Holding." *Human Systems Management* 27, no. 3, pp. 201–16.

Aycan, Z. 2008. "Cross-Cultural Perspectives to Work-Family Conflict." In *Handbook of Work-Family Conflict,* eds. K. Korabik, and D. Lero, 359–71. London: Cambrigde University Press.

Aycan, Z. 2006a. "Paternalizm: Towards Conceptual Refinement and Operationalization." In *Scientific Advances in Indigenous Psychologies: Empirical Philosophical and Cultural Contributions,* eds. K.-S. Yang, K.-K. Hwang, and U. Kim, 455–66. London: Sage.

Aycan, Z. 2006b. "Human Resource Management in Turkey." In *Managing Human Resources in the Middle East,* eds. P. Budhwar, and K. Mellahi, 160–80. New York: Routledge.

Aycan, Z. 2001. "Paternalizm: Yönetim ve Liderlik Anlayışına İlişkin Üç Görgül Çalışma (Paternalism: Three Empirical Studies Relating to Management and Leadership)." *Yönetim Araştırmaları Dergisi,* pp. 1–26.

Aycan, Z., R. Kanungo, M. Mendonca, K. Yu, J. Deller, G. Stahl, and A. Khursid. 2000. "Impact of Culture on Human Resource Management Practices: A Ten Country Comparison." *Applied Psychology: An International Review* 49, no. 1, pp. 192–220.

Aygün, Z.K., M. Arslan, and S. Güney. 2008. "Work Values of Turkish and American Students." *Journal of Business Ethics* 80, no. 2, pp. 205–23.

Bayiksel, Ş.Ö. 2009. "Ücrete Dikkat!" *Capital,* Retrieved from www.capital.com. tr/liderlik/ucrete-dikkat-haberdetay-5441 (accessed January 24, 2016).

Berkes, N. 1978. *Türkiye'de Çağdaşlaşma.* Istanbul: Doğu-Batı.

Bhasa, P.M. 2004. "Global Corporate Governance: Debates and Challenges." *Corporate Governance: The International Journal of Business in Society* 4, no. 2, pp. 5–17.

Bilgincan, M.C. 2015. *Ebediyeti Aramak: Hasan Güleşçi'nin Hayatı*. [Video]. accessed from www.youtube.com/watch?v=xW4w_c5KSTI

Bilgişin, M.Ş. 1936. *Türk Ticaret Hukuku Prensipleri*. Ankara: Ulus Basımevi.

Boratav, K., O. Türel, and E. Yeldan. 1996. "Dilemmas of Structural Adjustment and Environmental Policies under Instability: Post-1980 Turkey." *World Development* 24, no. 2, pp. 373–93.

Borsa İstanbul. 2015a. "Endeks Verileri." Retrieved from www.borsaistanbul.com/veriler/verileralt/endeks-verileri (accessed January 14, 2015).

Borsa İstanbul. 2015b. "İş Bankası ve İştiraklerinin Performansı Borsa İstanbul Tarafından Olçülecek." Retrieved from www.borsaistanbul.com/duyurular/2015/06/16/is-bankasi-ve-istiraklerinin-performansi-borsa-istanbul-tarafindan-olculecek (accessed July 28, 2015).

Borsa İstanbul. 2014a. "Kurumsal Yönetim Endeksi." Retrieved from www.borsaistanbul.com/endeksler/bist-pay-endeksleri/kurumsal-yonetim-endeksi (accessed January 14, 2015).

Borsa İstanbul. 2014b. "Borsa İstanbul, Halka Arz Calışmaları Kapsamında 500'üncü Sirket Ziyaretini Gerçekleştirdi." Retrieved from www.arkem.com.tr/Sites/1/upload/files/BIST_bb_halkaarz_500'uncusirket-7.pdf (accessed February 11, 2015).

Boston Consulting Group. 2006. "Türkiye Kurumsal Yönetim Haritası (Türkiye Kurumsal Yönetim Derneği)." Retrieved from www.tkyd.org/files/downloads/faaliyet_alanlari/yayinlarimiz/tkyd_yayinlari/bcgraporweb.pdf (accessed January 20, 2015).

Buğra, A. 1994. *State and Business in Modern Turkey: A Comparative Study*. New York: SUNY Press.

Burgan Bank. 2015. "Burgan Bank-Brief History." Retrieved from www.burgan.com.tr/about-us/brief-history (accessed October 15, 2015).

Capital Dergisi. 2002. "Oyak'ın A Takımı." Retrieved from www.capital.com.tr/sirketler-ve-yoneticiler/oyakin-a-takimi-haberdetay-2922 (accessed February 16, 2014).

Capital Market Board. 2015. "Mission statement." Retrieved from www.cmb.gov.tr/indexcont.aspx?action=showpage&menuid=0&pid=0&submenuheader=-1 (accessed February 2, 2015).

Çatalbaş, D. 2007. "Freedom of Press and Broadcasting." In *Human Rights Policies and Practices in Turkey*, ed. Z. Arat, 19–35. Philadelphia: Pennsylvania University Press.

Cebeci, T., and A.M. Fernandes. 2015. "Microdynamics of Turkey's Export Boom in the 2000s." *The World Economy* 38, no. 5, pp. 825–55.

Christensen, C. 2007. "Concentration of Ownership, The Fall of Unions and Government Legislation in Turkey." *Global Media and Communication* 3, no. 2, pp. 179–99.

Çiftçi, I. 2016. *Measuring the Effects of Ownership Structure and Board Attributes on Firm Performance: Evidence from Turkey.* Unpublished manuscript.

Çiftçi, M. 2011. "Osmanlı İmparatorluğu Döneminde Özel Mülkiyet ve Yapısal Özellikleri." *Turkish Studies,* pp. 623–44.

Claessens, S., S. Djankov, and L.H. Lang. 2000. "The Separation of Ownership and Control in East Asian Corporations." *Journal of Financial Economics* 58, no. 1, pp. 81–112.

Clark, E.C. 1969. *The Emergence of Textile Manufacturing Entrepreneurs in Turkey* 1804–1968. PhD diss, US: Princeton University.

Clarke, T. 2004. *Theories of Corporate Governance: The Theoretical Foundations.* Routledge: Abingdon.

Colpan, A.M. 2012. "Business Groups in Turkey." In *The Oxford Handbook of Business Groups,* eds. A. Colpan, T. Hikino, and J. Lincoln, 486–525. New York: Oxford University Press.

Colpan, A.M., and G. Jones. 2015. "Business Groups, Entrepreneurship and the Growth of the Koç Group in Turkey." *Business History.* doi: 10.1080/00076791.2015.1044521 (accessed February 15, 2016).

Dal, S., and Y.E. Çalış. 2013. "Anonim Şirketlerde Bağımsız Denetim, Bağımsız Denetçi." *Mali Çözüm,* pp. 87–106.

Davies, M., and B. Schlitzer. 2008. "The Impracticality of an International 'One Size Fits All.' Corporate Governance Code of Best Practice." *Managerial Auditing Journal* 23, no. 6, pp. 532–44.

De Jonghe, O., M. Disli, and K. Schoors. 2012. "Corporate Governance, Opaque Bank Activities, and Risk/Return Efficiency: Pre-And Post-Crisis Evidence From Turkey." *Journal of Financial Services Research* 41, nos. 1–2, pp. 51–80.

Demirağ, I., and M. Serter. 2003. "Ownership Patterns and Control in Turkish Listed Companies." *Corporate Governance: An International Review* 11, no. 1, pp. 40–51.

Doğuş Holding. 2015. "Doğuş Grubu Yönetim Kurulu." www.dogusgrubu.com. tr/tr/hakkimizda/yonetim-kurulu.aspx (accessed December 15, 2016).

Durukan, B., S. Ozkan, and F. Dalkilic. 2012. "CEO Turnover and Corporate Performance Relationship in Pre- and Post-IFRS Period: Evidence from Turkey." *Journal of Business Economics and Management* 13, no. 3, pp. 421–42.

Düzel, N. 2012. "Ünal Tekinalp: Patronlardan Hükümete Büyük Baskı Var." *Taraf,* May 28. Retrieved from www.hurhaber.com/nese-duzel/unal-tekinalp-patronlardan-hukumete-buyuk-baski-var/yazi-11164 (accessed November 20, 2014).

Eğilmez, M. 2015. "AKP'nin Ekonomide 12 yılı (12 years of AK Party in the Economy)." *Blog—Kendime Yazılar.* April 30. www.mahfiegilmez. com/2015/04/akpnin-ekonomide-13-yl.html

Ekonomi Bakanlığı. 2015a. Turkey and the EU. Retrieved from www.economy. gov.tr/portal/faces/home/disIliskiler/ulkeler/europe?_afrLoop=3824050 84826379&_afrWindowMode=0&_afrWindowId=1z4yuqcy t_414#!%40%40%3F_afrWindowId%3D1z4yuqcyt_414%26_ afrLoop%3D382405084826379%26_afrWindowMode%3D0%26_adf. ctrl-state%3D1z4yuqcyt_449 (accessed April 25, 2015).

Ekonomi Bakanlığı. 2015b. Regional initiatives. www.economy.gov.tr/ portal/faces/oracle/webcenter/portalapp/pages/content/htmlViewer.jspx?-contentId=UCM%23dDocName%3AEK-175732&parentPage=dis_ iliskiler&contentTitle=Regional%20Initiatives&countryName=&_ afrLoop=17114545544154&_afrWindowMode=0&_afrWin (accessed April 25, 2015).

Ekonomi Bakanlığı. 2012. "2023 Türkiye Ihracat Stratejisi, 2012." Retrieved from www.ekonomi.gov.tr/portal/content/conn/UCM/path/Contribution %20Folders/web/%C4%B0hracat/2023%20%C4%B0hracat%20 Stratejisi/2023-ihracat_stratejisi.pdf;jsessionid=3dO-wZYqj-BUjtB6LV5JAccaxJu-0CWS5gGY47ecVt_YCYKObpZ4i!75674881 (accessed February 26, 2015).

Elginkan Holding. 2016. "Vakfımızın Yapısı." Retrieved from www.elginkan. com.tr/tr/icerik/17/vakfimizin-yapisi (accessed January 23, 2016).

Elginkan Holding. 2004. "Foundation Voucher." Retrieved from www.elginkan. com.tr/en/content/393/foundation-voucher (accessed May 20, 2015).

Erçek, M. 2006. "HRMization in Turkey: Expanding the Rhetoric-Reality Debate in Space and Time." *International Journal of Human Resource Management* 17, no. 4, pp. 648–72.

Erçek, M., and Ö. Günçavdı. 2016. "Imprints of an Entrepreneur and Evolution of a Business Group 1948–2010." *Business History* 58, no. 1, pp. 89–110.

Ergur, A., S. Yamak, and M. Özbilgin. 2015. "Understanding the Nature of the Relationship Between the State and Business Elites." In *Research in the Sociology of Organizations: Elites on Trial,* eds. G. Morgan, S. Quack, and P. Hirsh, 107–30. London: Emerald.

Ergüder, Ü., Y. Esmer, and E. Kalaycıoğlu. 1991. *Türk Toplumunun Değerleri.* Istanbul: TÜSİAD.

Ertuna, B. 2013. "Corporate Social Responsibility: Interaction Between Market and Community." In *A Companion to Organizational Anthropology,* eds. D. Caulkins and A. Jordan, 438–54. West Sussex: Blackwell Publishing Limited.

Ertuna, B., and A. Tükel. 2013. "Do Foreign Institutional Investors Reward Transparency and Disclosure: Evidence from Istanbul Stock Exchange." *Journal of Emerging Market Finance* 12, no. 1, pp. 31–57.

Ertuna, B., and A. Tükel. 2007. "Board Composition and Control Mechanisms in ISE50: Form Outscores Substance." Paper presented at the ECGI Corporate Governance in Emerging Markets, Istanbul, Sabancı University.

Ertuna, B., M. Ercan, and V. Akgiray. 2003. "The Effect of the Issuer Underwriter Relationship on Ipos: The Case of an Emerging Market." *Journal of Entrepreneurial Finance and Business Ventures* 8, no. 3, pp. 43–55.

Ertuna, B., and S. Yamak. 2011. "Foreign Equity Configurations in an Emerging Country: Implications for Performance." *European Management Journal* 29, no. 2, pp. 117–28.

Ertürk, I. 2003. "Governance of Financialisation: The Turkish Case." *Competition and Change* 7, no. 4, pp. 185–204.

Esirgen, S.Ö. 2011. "Osmanlı Devleti'nde Medeni Kanun Tartışmaları: Mecelle mi Fransız Medeni Kanunu mu?" *Ankara Üniversitesi Osmanlı Tarihi Araştırma ve Uygulama Merkezi Dergisi* 29, no. 29, pp. 31–48.

Esmer, Y. 2012. *Türkiye Değerler Araştırması 2012, Istanbul: Bahçeşehir Üniversitesi.* Retrieved from http://bahcesehir.edu.tr/icerik/1725-turkiye-degerler-atlasi-2012-yayinlandi (accessed August 08, 2014).

European Commission. 2014. "Enterprise and Industry: 2014 SBA Fact Sheet Turkey." Retrieved from file:///C:/Users/Administrator/Downloads/turkey_en%20(2).pdf (accessed June 15, 2015).

EÜAŞ. 2010. "EÜAŞ Elektrik Üretim A.Ş.: Hakkımızda, 2015." Retrieved from www.euas.gov.tr/Sayfalar/Hakk%C4%B1m%C4%B1zda.aspx (accessed June 15, 2015).

Family Business Advisors. 2007. "Kurumsallaşma Devir Teslim: Devrederken Devrilmemek İçin." Retrieved from http://family-advisor.com/press/article/2007_CNBC_Business_Devreden_Devrilmemek_icin.pdf (accessed May 4, 2015).

Forbes. 2016. "The World's 100 Most Powerful Women." Retrieved from www.forbes.com/power-women/#tab:overall_country:Turkey (accessed May 26, 2016).

Ford Otosan. 2015. "Ford Otosan Yatırımcı Ilişkileri." Retrieved from www.fordotosan.com.tr/downloads/yatirimciiliskileri/30_06_2015%20Mali%20Tablolar%20ve%20Dipnotlar.pdf (accessed September 15, 2015).

Fortune. 2016. "Fortune 500—2016." Retrieved from www.fortuneturkey.com/fortune500 (accessed January 22, 2016).

Freedom House. 2014a. "Country Report: Turkey." Retrieved from https://freedomhouse.org/report/freedom-net/2014/turkey (accessed December 4, 2014).

Freedom House. 2014b. "Democracy in Crisis: Corruption, Media and Power in Turkey." Retrieved from https://freedomhouse.org/report/democracy-crisis-corruption-media-and-power-turkey/media-ownership-and-dependency#.VIHUqpX8Iad (accessed November 30, 2014).

Freedom House. 2015. "Country Report: Turkey." Retrieved from https://freedomhouse.org/report/freedom-net/2015/turkey (accessed February 24, 2016).

Genckaya, O., S. Togan, and L. Schulz. 2015. *Sustainable Governance Indicators: 2015 Turkey Report.* Gütersloh, Germany: Bertelsmann Stiftung.

Gilson, R.J. 2004. "Globalizing Corporate Governance: Convergence in Form or Function." In *Convergence and Persistence in Corporate Governance,* eds. J.N. Gordon, and M.J. Roe, 128–58. Cambridge: Cambridge University Press.

Gönenç, R., O. Röhn, V. Koen, and F. Öğünç. 2014. Structural Change in the Business Sector (OECD Economics Department Working Papers No.1161). France: OECD Publishing.

Gözütok, N. 2010. "Süper Ücretli CEO'lar." *Capital,* Retrieved from www.capital.com.tr/capital-dergi/super-ucretli-ceolar-haberdetay-5965 (accessed January 23, 2016).

Gros, D., and C. Selçuki. 2013. *The Changing Structure of Turkey's Trade and Industrial Competitiveness.* Brussels: Center for European Policy Studies.

Grosvold, J. 2011. "Where are All the Women? Institutional Context and the Prevalence of Women on the Corporate Board of Directors." *Business and Society,* pp. 531–55.

Gugler, K., D.C. Mueller, and B.B. Yurtoglu. 2008. "Insider Ownership, Ownership Concentration and Investment Performance: An International Comparison." *Journal of Corporate Finance* 14, no. 5, pp. 688–705.

Guillen, M.F. 2001. *The Limits of Convergence: Globalization and Organizational Change in Argentina, South Korea, and Spain.* New Jersey: Princeton University Press.

Gursoy, G., and K. Aydoğan. 2002. "Equity Ownership Structure, Risk Taking and Performance." *Emerging Markets Finance and Trade* 38, no. 6, pp. 6–25.

Güler, H. 2015. "Ekonomi: Koç Holding." *Hürriyet Gazetesi.* Retrieved from www.hurriyet.com.tr/torunu-koc-a-gobekten-bagladik-28712352 (accessed May 20, 2015).

Herbert Smith Freehills Dispute Resolution. 2015. "Cukurova v Sonera: Privy Council Dismisses Backdoor Attempt to Challenge Tribunal's Findings at the Enforcement Stage." Retrieved from http://hsfnotes.com/arbitration/2014/05/23/cukurova-v-sonera-privy-council-dismisses-backdoor-attempt-to-challenge-tribunals-findings-at-the-enforcement-stage/ (accessed February 19, 2015).

Herdem, Ş. 2013. *Turkey: A Corporate Guide for Private Equity Funds in Turkey: Board of Directors in Joint Stock Companies.* Istanbul: Mondaq Business Briefing.

Hofstede, G. 2001. *Culture's Consequences: Comparing Values, Behaviors, Institutions and Organizations Across Nations.* Thousand Oaks: Sage.

Hofstede, G. 1980. *Culture's Consequences: International Differences in Work Related Values.* Beverly Hills, CA: Sage.

Hoskisson, R.E., M. Wright, I. Filatotchev, and M.W. Peng. 2013. "Emerging Multinational from Mid-range Economies: The Influence of Institutions and Factor Markets." *Journal of Management Studies* 50, pp. 1295–321.

Hürriyet Gazetesi. 2015. "Borsa'dan 80 Şirket İSO 500'e Girdi." Retrieved from www.hurriyet.com.tr/ekonomi/29298993.asp (accessed June 17, 2015).

IIF EAG. 2005. "Corporate Governance in Turkey: An Investor Perspective." Retrieved from http://forecasturkey.com/Articles/Multilateral%20Agencies/international%20agencies/IIF/IIFCorpGovTurkey_0405.pdf (accessed February 26, 2015).

IMF. 2016. "World GDP Ranking 2016." Retrieved from http://knoema.com/nwnfkne/world-gdp-ranking-2015-data-and-charts (accessed January 30, 2016).

İstanbul Chamber of Industry. 2015. "Türkiyenin 500 Büyük Sanayi Kuruluşu." Retrieved from www.iso.org.tr/projeler/turkiyenin-500-buyuk-sanayi-kurulusu (accessed December 2, 2015).

İstanbul Chamber of Industry. 2014. "Türkiye'nin 500 Büyük Sanayi Kuruluşu." Retrieved from www.iso.org.tr/Sites/1/content/500-buyuk-liste.html?j=6493030 (accessed May 20, 2015).

İstanbul Chamber of Industry. 2010. *Türkiye'nin 500 Büyük Sanayi Kuruluşu.* İstanbul: İstanbul Sanayi Odası.

İlkin, S. 1971. "Türkiye Milli Ithalat ve Ihracat Anonim Şirketi." *ODTÜ Gelişme Dergisi* 2, pp. 199–233.

İnalcık, H. 1998. "Turkey between Europe and the Middle East." *Journal of International Affairs* 3, no. 1. Retrieved from www.sam.gov.tr/wp-content/uploads/2012/02/HalilInalcik.pdf (accessed January 30, 2015).

İş Bankası. 2015. "İştiraklerimiz." Retrieved from www.isbank.com.tr/TR/hakkimizda/bizi-taniyin/istiraklerimiz/Sayfalar/istiraklerimiz.aspx (accessed June 21, 2015).

İş Bankası. 2014. "Türkiye İş Bankası 2014 Faaliyet Raporu." Retrieved from www.isbank.com.tr/TR/hakkimizda/yatirimci-iliskileri/finansal-bilgiler/yillik-ve-ara-donem-faaliyet-raporlari/Documents/FaaliyetRaporu2014.pdf (accessed March 22, 2015).

Kabasakal, H., and M. Bodur. 2007. "Leadership and Culture in Turkey: A Multifaceted Phenomenon." In *Culture and Leadership across the World: The Globe Book of In-Depth Studies of 25 Countries*, eds. S.C. Jagdeep, C.B. Felix, and J.H. Robert, 835–74. London: Lawrence ERbaum Associates.

Kalder. 2015. "Turgay Durak." Retrieved from www.kalder.org: www.kalder.org/TumResimler/turgaydurak.pdf (accessed December 15, 2015).

KAP. 2016a. "Al Baraka Türk Katılım Bankası: Kamuyu Aydınlatma Platformu." Retrieved from www.kap.gov.tr/en/companies/traded-companies/all-companies/detail.aspx?sId=1467 (accessed January 25, 2016).

KAP. 2016b. "Denizbank: Kamuyu Aydınlatma Platformu." Retrieved from www.kap.gov.tr/en/companies/traded-companies/all-companies/detail.aspx?sId=1394 (accessed January 25, 2016).

KAP. 2015a. "İlgili Mevzuat ve Düzenlemeler." Retrieved from www.kap.gov.tr/mevzuat-ve-sistem-kullanimi/ilgili-mevzuat-ve-duzenlemeler.aspx (accessed January 14, 2015).

KAP. 2015b. "Ford Otomotiv Sanayi A.Ş." Retrieved from http://kap.gov.tr/sirketler/islem-goren-sirketler/tum-sirketler/detay.aspx?sId=956 (accessed October 7, 2015).

KAP. 2015c. "General Assembly Invitation-Turkcell." Retrieved from www.kap.gov.tr/en/search/notice-results.aspx?id=412767 (accessed February 15, 2015).

KAP. 2015d. "Türkiye Garanti Bankası A.Ş." Retrieved from www.kap.gov.tr/sirketler/islem-goren-sirketler/tum-sirketler/detay.aspx?sId=1081 (accessed October 15, 2015).

Karabag, S.F., and C. Berggren. 2014. "Antecedents of Firm Performance in Emerging Economies: Business Groups, Strategy, Industry Structure, and State Support." *Journal of Business Research* 67, no. 10, pp. 2212–23.

Keyman, E.F, and B. Koyuncu. 2005. "Globalization, Alternative Modernities and the Political Economy of Turkey." *Review of International Political Economy* 12, no. 1, pp. 105–28.

Koç Holding. 2015a. *Koç Basın Bülteni: Koç Holding*. Retrieved from www.koc.com.tr/en-us/koc-agenda/media-center/PressRelease/Koc-Holding-BB-17-Feb-2015_en.pdf (accessed February 17, 2015a).

Koç Holding. 2015b. *Levent Çakıroğlu*. Retrieved from www.koc.com.tr/tr-tr/hakkinda/organizasyon-semasi/Sayfalar/levent-cakiroglu.aspx (accessed December 15, 2015b).

Koç, V. 1991. *Recollections, Observations, Counsel*. Istanbul: Vehbi Koç Foundation.

Koç, V. 1983. *Hayat Hikayem*. Istanbul: Çeltik Matbaacılık.

Kort, M. 2008. "Standardization of Company Law in Germany, other EU Member States and Turkey by Corporate Governance Rules." *European Company and Financial Law Review* 5, no. 4, pp. 379–421.

Kula, V. 2005. "The Impact of the Roles, Structure and Process of Boards on Firm Performance: Evidence from Turkey." *Corporate Governance: An International Review* 13, no. 2, pp. 265–76.

Kuyucak, H.A. 1939. *Ticaret Hukuku*. Istanbul: Marif Vekilliği Siyasal Bilgiler Okulu Yayınları.

Küçükgüngör, M.A. 2014. "Harmonization of Turkish Law with the European Union Legislation in the Area of Financial Markets Infrastructure: The New Capital Markets Law." *Uniform Law Review* 19, no. 1, pp. 88–105.

La Porta, R., F. Lopez-de-Silanes, and A. Shleifer. 2008. "The Economic Consequences of Legal Origins." *Journal of Economic Literature* 46, no. 2, pp. 285–332.

La Porta, R., F. Lopez-de-Silanes, and A. Shleifer. 1999. "Corporate Ownership Around the World." *Journal of Finance* 54, no. 2, pp. 471–517.

La Porta, R., F. Lopez-de-Silanes, A. Shleifer, and R. Vishny. 2002. "Investor Protection and Corporate Valuation." *Journal of Finance* 57, no. 3, pp. 1147–70.

La Porta, R., F. Lopez-de-Silanes, A. Shleifer, and R. Vishny. 1998. "Law and Finance." *Journal of Political Economy* 106, pp. 1113–55.

Leuz, C., K.V. Lins, and F.E. Warnock. 2009. "Do Foreigners Invest Less in Poorly Governed Firms." *The Review of Financial Studies* 22, no. 8, pp. 3245–85.

Licht, A.N. 2000. "The Mother of All Path Dependencies: Toward a Cross-Cultural Theory of Corporate Governance Systems." *SSRN Electronic Journal,* accessed from SSRN 208489.

Mandacı, P., and G. Gumus. 2010. "Ownership Concentration, Managerial Ownership and Firm Performance: Evidence from Turkey." *South East European Journal of Economics and Business* 5, no. 1, pp. 57–66.

Manktelow, A, ed. 2014. *Guide to Emerging Markets: The Business Outlook, Opportunities and Obstacles.* London: The Economist Profile Books Ltd.

Marois, T. 2012. *States, Banks and Crises: Emerging Finance Capitalism in Mexico and Turkey.* Cheltenham, UK: Edward Elgar.

Milhaupt, C.J. 2004. "Property Rights in Firms." In *Convergence and Persistence in Corporate Governance,* eds. J.N. Gordon, and M.J. Roe, 21–51. Cambridge: Cambridge University Press.

Ministry of Labour and Social Security. 2014. *National Employment Strategy 2014–2013.* Ankara: Ministry of Labour and Social Security and General Directorate of Labour.

Nebil, F.S. 2015. "6 Milyar Lira Harcama Kapasiteli Turkcell'de Yeni CEO Kim Olur?" *T24 Bağımsız İnternet Gazetesi.* Retrieved from http://t24.com.tr/yazarlar/fusun-sarp-nebil/6-milyar-lira-harcama-kapasiteli-turkcellde-yeni-ceo-kim-olur,11210 (accessed February 20, 2015).

Nilsson, G.O. 2007. "Corporate Governance in Turkey." *European Business Organization Law Review* 8, no. 2, pp. 195–236.

Oba, B., E. Tigrel, and P. Sener. 2014. "Board Structure in Listed Firms: Evidence From an Emerging Economy." *Corporate Governance* 14, no. 3, pp. 382–94.

Oba, B., Z. Özsoy, and S. Atakan. 2010. "Power in the Boardroom: A Study on Turkish Family-Owned and Listed Companies." *Corporate Governance* 10, no. 5, pp. 603–16.

OECD. 2014. *Phase 3 Report on Implementing The OECD Anti Bribery Convention in Turkey*. Paris: OECD.

OECD. 2013. "Corporate Governance: Supervision and Enforcement in Corporate Governance." Retrieved from http://dx.doi.org/10.1787/9789264203334-en (accessed September 9, 2014).

OECD. 2006. *Corporate Governance in Turkey: A Pilot Study*. Paris: OECD Publishing.

Oktar, O. 2007. "İş Dünyasında Silahlı Kuvvetler." Master's diss, Pamukkale Üniversitesi, Denizli.

Orbay, H., and B. Yurtoğlu. 2006. "The Impact of Corporate Governance Structures on the Corporate Investment Performance in Turkey." *Corporate Governance: An International Review* 14, no. 4, pp. 349–63.

OVM Petrol Ofisi. 2016. "Yönetim Kurulu." Retrieved from www.omvpetrolofisiholding.com.tr/hakkimizda-yonetim-kurulu.html (accessed January 25, 2016).

OYAK. 2016. "OYAK Kanunu." Retrieved from www.oyak.com.tr/TR/kurumsal/oyak-nedir/oyak-kanunu.html (accessed January 25, 2016).

OYAK. 2015. "Genel Müdürün Mesajı." Retrieved from www.oyak.com.tr/TR/kurumsal/genel-mudur-un-mesaji.html (accessed December 31, 2015).

OYAK. 2014. "Annual Report." Retrieved from http://content.oyak.com.tr/oyakdosyalar/media/editor/files/CORPORATE/annual-reports/OYAK_AnnualReport2014.PDF (accessed March 22, 2015).

OYAK. 1961. "Military Personnel Assistance (and Pension) Fund Law, 1961." www.oyak.com.tr/EN/corporate/what-oyak-is/law-of-oyak.html (accessed June 11, 2015).

Ozkan, S., C.K Balsari, and S. Varan. 2014. "Effect of Banking Regulation on Performance: Evidence from Turkey." *Emerging Markets Finance and Trade* 50, no. 4, pp. 196–211.

Öncü, A. 2013. "Television and Media." In *The Routledge Handbook of Modern Turkey*, eds. M. Heper, and S. Sayarı, 125–36. New York: Routledge.

Öniş, Z., and F. Şenses. 2007. *Global Dynamics, Domestic Coalitions and a Reactive State: Major Policy Shifts in Post-War Turkish Economic Development*. Ankara: Turkish Economic Association.

Özbilgin, M. 2011. "Leadership in Turkey: Towards an Evidence Based and Contextual Approach." *Leadership Development in the Middle East*, pp. 275–89.

Özcan, G.B., and M. Çokgezen. 2003. "Limits to Alternative Forms of Capitalization: The Case of Anatolian Holding Companies." *World Development* 31, no. 12, pp. 2061–84.

Özer, M.H. 2014. "Cumhuriyetin İlk Yıllarında Milli Tüccar Oluşturma Çabalarında İş Bankasıʾnın Rolü." *Ankara Üniversitesi SBF Dergisi* 69, no. 2, pp. 351–77.

Pamuk, Ş. 2014. *Türkiye'nin 200 Yıllık İktisadi Tarihi: Büyüme, Kurumlar ve Bölüşüm*. İstanbul: Türkiye İş Bankası Kültür Yayınları.

Peker, E., and Y. Candemir. 2015. "Turkey's 2014 GDP Below Official Expectations." *Wall Street Journal*. Retrieved from www.wsj.com/articles/turkeys-2014-gdp-below-official-expectations-1427817362 (accessed April 30, 2015).

PEN International. 2016. "Can Dündar Writes from Prison." Retrieved from www.pen-international.org/newsitems/can-dundar-writes-from-prison/ (accessed January 27, 2016).

Peryön and Towers Watson. 2014. "İş Gücü Analitikleri: Çalışan Devir Oranı Araştırması." Retrieved from http://peryonkongre.com/peryon/pdf/PERYON_TW_CALISAN_DEVIR_ORANI_ARASTIRMA_RAPORU_6AY2013.pdf (accessed January 30, 2015).

Pesqueux, Y., S. Yamak, and O. Süer. 2004. Les Scandales Bancaires Au Prisme de l'éthique: Une Comparaison Franco-Turque. Working paper. Paris: IAE Sorbonne.

Poroy, R. 1988. "Son Elli Yılda Türkiye'de Kara Ticareti Hukuku Alanındaki Kanunlaştırma Hareketinin Genel Teori Açısından Değerlendirilmesi." Paper presented at Türk Ticaret Kanunu'nun 30. Yıl Semineri, İstanbul.

Privatization Administration. 2016. "Companies in the Privatization Portfolio." Retrieved from www.oib.gov.tr/portfoy/portfolio_general.htm (accessed June 15, 2015).

PTT. 2016. "Yönetim Kurulu." Retrieved from http://ptt.gov.tr/ptt/ (accessed January 23, 2016).

Public Oversight, Accounting and Auditing Standards Authority. 2015. "Our duties." Retrieved from www.kgk.gov.tr/contents/files/our_duties.pdf (accessed May 22, 2015).

Reporters Without Borders. 2016. "World Press Freedom Index." Retrieved from https://rsf.org/en/ranking (accessed February 24, 2016).

Resmi Gazete. 2012. "Türk Ticaret Kanunu ile Türk Ticaret Kanunu'nun Yürürlüğü ve Uygulama Şekli Hakkında Kanunda Değişiklik Yapılmasına Dair Kanun." Retrieved from www.resmigazete.gov.tr/eskiler/2012/06/20120630-5.htm (accessed March 20, 2015).

Rethink Institute. 2014. *Diminishing Press Freedom in Turkey*, p. 1. Washington DC.

Roos, L.L., and N.P. Roos. 1971. *Managers of Modernization: Organizations and Elites in Turkey*. Cambridge, MA: Harvard University Press.

Sabancı, S. 1985. İşte Hayatım. Istanbul: Aksoy Yayınları.

Sabancı Group. 2016. "Board of Directors." Retrieved from www.sabanci.com/en/sabanci-group/board-of-directors,-sbu-presidents-and-corporate-management/k-58 (accessed January 25, 2016).

Şanda, H.A. 1978. *1908 İşçi Hareketleri:Yarı Müstemleke Oluş Tarihi.* İstanbul: Gözlem Yayınları.

Şaylan, G. 1974. *Turkiye'de Kapitalizm, Bürokrasi ve Siyasal Ideoloji.* Ankara: TODAIE.

Schwartz, S.H. 1994. "Beyond Individualism: New Cultural Dimensions of Values." In *Individualism and Collectivism: Theory, Methods and Applications,* eds. U. Kim, H. Triandis, Ç. Kagitçibasi, S.-C. Choi, and G. Yoon, 85–119. Thousand Oaks, CA: Sage.

Selekler-Göksen, N., and A. Karatas. 2008. "Board Structure and Performance in an Emerging Economy: Turkey." *International Journal of Business Governance and Ethics* 4, no. 2, pp. 132–47.

Selekler-Gökşen, N., and B. Üsdiken. 2001. "Uniformity and Diversity in Turkish Business Groups: Effects of Scale and Time of Founding." *British Journal of Management* 12, no. 4, pp. 325–40.

Selekler-Göksen, N., and Ö. Yildirim-Öktem. 2009. "Countervailing Institutional Forces: Corporate Governance in Turkish Family Business Groups." *Journal of Management and Governance* 13, no. 3, pp. 193–213.

Sermaye Piyasası Kurulu. 2015. "Kurumsal Yönetim Ilkelerinin Belirlenmesine ve Uygulanmasına Ilişkin Tebliğ." Retrieved from www.spk.gov.tr/displayfile.aspx?action=displayfile&pageid=66&fn (accessed September 17, 2015).

Sermaye Piyasası Kurulu. 2014. "Communique on Corporate Governance." Retrieved from www.cmb.gov.tr/apps/teblig/displayteblig.aspx?id=479&ct=f&action=displayfile (accessed March 15, 2015).

Solomon, J., and A. Solomon. 2004. "The Role of Transparency in Corporate Governance." *Corporate Governance and Accountability, John Wiley & Sons, Ltd,* pp. 119–43.

Sonmez, M. 2014. "The Role of Better Transparency Law in Corporate Governance and Financial Markets, and Its Practicability in Legal Systems: A Comparative Study Between the EU and Turkey." PhD diss., Durham University.

Stiftung, B. 2016. "Sustainable Governance Indicators." Retrieved from www.sgi-network.org/2015/Turkey (accessed January 29, 2016).

Sustainable Governance Indicators. 2015. "2015 Turkey Report." Retrieved from www.sgi-network.org/docs/2015/country/SGI2015_Turkey.pdf (accessed May 22, 2015).

Tatoglu, E., V. Kula, and K.W. Glaister. 2008. "Succession Planning in Family Owned Businesses: Evidence from Turkey." *International Small Business Journal* 26, no. 2, pp. 155–80.

TCDD. 2014. "Faaliyet Raporu." Retrieved from www.tcdd.gov.tr/files/istatistik/2014faaliyetraporu.pdf (accessed January 25, 2016).

TCDD. 2016. "Organizasyon Şeması." www.tcdd.gov.tr/organizasyon-semasi+m75 (accessed January 23, 2016).

TETAŞ. 2016. "Yönetim Kadrosu: Türkiye Elektrik Ticaret ve Taahhüt A.Ş." Retrieved from www.tetas.gov.tr/tr-TR/Yonetim-Kadrosu (accessed January 23, 2016).

Tezel, Y. 2002. *Cumhuriyet Döneminin İktisadi Tarihi.* Istanbul: Tarih Vakfı Yayınları.

The Economist. 2012. "Turkish Corporate Governance: The Battle for Turkcell 2012." April 19. Retrieved from www.economist.com/node/21553054 (accessed April 6, 2015).

The Economist. 2013. "The Press in Turkey: Not so free 2013." April 4. Retrieved from www.economist.com/news/europe/21575823-government-finds-different-ways-intimidate-free-media-not-so-free (accessed April 6, 2015).

The Economist. 2014a. "Turkey and the European Union." December 20. Retrieved from www.economist.com/news/europe/21636764-fresh-round-arrests-takes-relations-european-union-new-low-media-freedom-rip (accessed March 1, 2015).

The Economist. 2014b. "Turkish Conglomerates: Too Big to Fail, But in a Good Way." January 30. Retrieved from www.economist.com/news/business/21595463-two-huge-family-firms-koc-and-sabanci-should-weather-turkeys-crisis-too-big-fail (accessed March 1, 2014).

Timur, T. 1989. *Osmanlı Çalışmaları (Ottoman Studies).* Ankara: Verso.

Toprak, Z. 1995a. *Türkiye'de Ekonomi ve Toplum (1908–1950): İttihat ve Terakki ve Devletçilik.* Istanbul: Tarih Vakfı.

Toprak, Z. 1995b. *Türkiye'de Ekonomi ve Toplum (1908–1950): Milli İktisat Milli Burjuvazi.* Istanbul: Tarih Vakfı,

Transparency International. 2015. "Turkey and Western Balkans: National integrity systems." Retrieved from http://archive.transparency.org/regional_pages/europe_central_asia/projects_and_activities/cimap (accessed February 2, 2015).

Trompenaars, F., and C. Hampden-Turner. 1998. *Riding The Waves of the Culture.* New York: McGraw-Hill.

Tuan, K., and E. Arıoğlu. 2014. "The State of Independent Auditing in the Turkish Commercial Code." *Journal of Economics Finance and Accounting* 1, no. 1, pp. 46–58.

TÜİK (Turkish Statistical Institute). 2015a. "Adrese Dayalı Nüfus Kayıt Sistemi Sonuçları." Retrieved from www.tuik.gov.tr/PreHaberBultenleri.do?id=21507 (accessed January 30, 2016).

TÜİK (Turkish Statistical Institute). 2015b. "Ulusal Hesaplar." Retrieved from www.tuik.gov.tr/UstMenu.do?metod=temelist (accessed May 19, 2015).

TÜİK (Turkish Statistical Institute). 2014. "Temel Istatistikler, Yıllara Göre Dış Ticaret." Retrieved from www.tuik.gov.tr/UstMenu.do?metod=temelist (accessed March 22, 2015).

TÜPRAŞ. 2016. "About TÜPRAŞ/Board Of Directors." Retrieved from www.tupras.com.tr/en/board-of-directors (accessed January 25, 2016).

TÜSİAD. 2014. "Kurumsal Yönetim Ilkeleri." Retrieved from www.tusiad.org/tr/yayinlar/raporlar/item/1861-kurumsal-yonetim-ilkeleri (accessed December 12, 2014).

Türk Ticaret Kanunu. 2011. "Türk Ticaret Kanunu." Retrieved from www.ticaretkanunu.net/wp-content/uploads/2012/08/6102-TTK.pdf (accessed February 25, 2015).

TÜYİD and MKK. 2015. "Borsa Trendleri Raporu: Ocak-Aralık 2014 (sayı 11,)." Retrieved from www.mkk.com.tr/project/MKK/file/content/Bilgi%20Merkezi%20Dosyalar%C4%B1%2FBorsa%20Trendleri%20Raporu%2FBorsa%20Trendleri%20Raporu%20XI (accessed May 19, 2015).

Uğur, M., and M. Ararat. 2006. "Does Macroeconomic Performance Affect Corporate Governance: Evidence from Turkey." *Corporate Governance: An International Review*, pp. 325–48.

Ülengin, F., Ö. Kabak, Ş. Önsel, E. Aktaş, and B.R. Parker. 2011. "The Competitiveness of Nations and Implications for Human Development." *Soci-Economic Planning Sciences* 45, pp. 16–27.

Undersecretariat of Treasury. 2015. "Turkish Economy." Retrieved from www.treasury.gov.tr/en-US/Pages/Turkish-Economy (accessed June 15, 2015).

UNDP. 2014. *Human Development Report 2014 Sustaining Human Progress: Reducing Vulnerability and Building Resilience*. New York: PBM Graphics, an RR Donnelley Company.

United Nations Refugee Agency. 2016. "Syria Regional Refugee Response." Retrieved from http://data.unhcr.org/syrianrefugees/country.php?id=224 (accessed February 10, 2016).

U.S. Department of State Bureau of Democracy, Human Rights and Labor. 2015. International Religious Freedom Report. Retrieved from www.state.gov/j/drl/rls/irf/religiousfreedom/index.htm#wrapper (accessed February 9, 2014).

Üsdiken, B. 2008. "Türkiye'de Işletme Grupları: Özel Sayıya Giriş (Business Groups in Turkey: Introduction)." *Yönetim Araştırmaları Dergisi*, pp. 5–21.

Üsdiken, B., and Ö. Yildirim-Öktem. 2008. "Kurumsal Ortamda Değişim ve Büyük Aile Holdingleri Bünyesindeki Şirketlerin Yönetim Kurullarında 'Icrada Görevli Olmayan' ve 'Bağımsız Üyeler.'" *Amme İdaresi Dergisi*, pp. 43–71.

West, A. 2009. "Corporate Governance Convergence and Moral Relativism." *Corporate Governance: An International Review* 17, no. 1, pp. 107–19.

Whitley, R. 1994. "Dominant Forms of Economic Organization in Market Economies." *Organisation Studies* 15, no. 2, pp. 153–82.

World Bank. 2016a. *Urban Population (% of Total)*. Retrieved from http://data.worldbank.org/indicator/SP.URB.TOTL.IN.ZS (accessed February 11, 2016).

World Bank. 2016b. *Trading up to High Income: Turkey Country Economic Memorandum* (Report Number 82307-TR). Retrieved from http://documents.worldbank.org/curated/en/924601468121739356/pdf/823070REPLACEM00Box385262B00PUBLIC0.pdf (accessed February 11, 2016).

World Bank. 2014a. *Doing Business in 2015: Economy Profile 2015-Turkey*. Washington DC: The World Bank.

World Bank. 2014b. *Evaluation of the EU-Turkey Customs Union*. Washington DC: World Bank Publications.

World Bank. 2014c. *Turkey's Transitions: Integration, Inclusion, Institutions*. Washington DC: World Bank Publications.

World Bank. 2015. *World Development Indicators, Data, Turkey 2014*. Retrieved from http://data.worldbank.org/country/turkey (accessed May 19, 2015).

*Worldwide Governance Indicators*. 2014. World Bank: *Country Data Report for Turkey: 1996–2014*. Retrieved from http://info.worldbank.org/governance/wgi/index.aspx#countryReports (accessed June 8, 2014).

World Bank. 2013. *Country Partnership Strategy for the Republic of Turkey for the Period 2012–2015*. Washington DC: World Bank Publications.

World Economic Forum. 2014. *The Global Competitiveness Report 2014–2015*. Geneva: World Economic Forum.

World Economic Forum. 2004. *Global Competitiveness Report 2004/2005*. Geneva: World Economic Forum.

World Trade Organization. 2014. "Trade Profiles—Turkey." Retrieved from http://stat.wto.org/CountryProfile/WSDBCountryPFView.aspx?Language=E&Country=TR (accessed April 25, 2015).

Yamak, S. 1996. "Managerial Backgrounds in Large Enterprises in Turkey: The Impact Of Strategy, Context and Organizational Attributes." PhD diss., Boğaziçi University.

Yamak, S. 2006. "Changing Institutional Environment and Business Elites in Turkey." *Society and Business Review* 1, no. 3, pp. 206–19.

Yamak, S., and B. Ertuna. 2010. *Ownership Characteristics of Turkish Companies: Changes from 1999 to 2009*. Unpublished manuscript.

Yamak, S., and B. Ertuna. 2012. "Corporate Governance and Initial Public Offerings in Turkey." In *Corporate Governance and Initial Public Offerings: An International Perspective*, eds. A. Zattoni, and W. Judge, 470–98. Cambridge: Cambridge University Press.

Yamak, S., and A. Ergur. 2014. *Türk İş Dünyasında Seçkinler.* Unpublished Paper.

Yamak, S., and B. Üsdiken. 2006. "Economic Liberalization and the Antecedents of Top Management Teams: Evidence from Turkish 'Big' Business." *British Journal of Management* 17, no. 3, pp. 177–94.

Yamak, S., B. Ertuna, and M. Bolak. 2006. "Sahiplik Dağılımının Birleşik Liderlik Yapısı Üzerine Etkileri." *Yönetim Araştırmaları Dergisi* 6, pp. 85–105.

Yamak, S., B. Ertuna, H. Levent, and M. Bolak. 2015. "Collaboration of Foreign Investors with Local Family Business Groups in Turkey: Implications on Firm Performance." *European Journal of International Management*, pp. 263–81.

Yamak, S., A. Ergur, O.N. Alakavuklar, and M. Özbilgin. 2016. "Gender as Symbolic Capital and Violence: The Case of Corporate Elites in Turkey." *Gender, Work and Organization* 23, no. 2, pp. 125–46.

Yamak, S., A. Ergur, A. Ünsal, S. Uygur, and M. Özbilgin. 2015. "Between a Rock and a Hard Place: Corporate Elites in the Context of Religion and Secularism in Turkey." *International Journal of Human Resource Management* 26, no. 11, pp. 1474–97.

Yanardağoğlu, E. 2013. "Elusive Citizenship: Media, Minorities and Freedom of Communication in Turkey in the Last Decade." *İletişim* 19, pp. 87–102.

Yeginsu, C. 2015. "Opposition Journalists Under Assault in Turkey." *The New York Times*, September 17.

Yildirim-Öktem, Ö., and B. Üsdiken. 2010. "Contingencies Versus External Pressure: Professionalization in Boards of Firms Affiliated to Family Business Groups in Late-industrializing Countries." *British Journal of Management* 21, no. 1, pp. 115–30.

Yildirim-Öktem, Ö., and B. Üsdiken. 2007. "Reconciling Family-centric and Professionalized Governance: Boards of Firms within Family Business Groups." Paper presented at the Academy of Management Best Papers Proceedings, Philadelphia: AoM.

Yoshikawa, T., and A.A. Rasheed. 2009. "Convergence of Corporate Governance: Critical Review and Future Directions." *Corporate Governance: An International Review* 17, no. 3, pp. 388–404.

Yurtoğlu, B. 2003. "Corporate Governance and Implications for Minority Shareholders in Turkey." *Journal of Corporate Ownership and Control* 1, no. 1, pp. 72–86.

Yurtoğlu, B. 2000. "Ownership, Control and Performance of Turkish Listed Firms." *Empirica* 27, no. 2, pp. 193–222.

# Index

## OTHER TITLES IN THE CORPORATE GOVERNANCE COLLECTION

William Q. Judge and Kenneth Merchant, University of Southern California, Editors

- *A Director's Guide to Corporate Financial Reporting* by Kristen Fiolleau, Kris Hoang and Karim Jamal
- *Blind Spots, Biases, and Other Pathologies in the Boardroom* by Kenneth Merchant and Katharina Pick
- *A Primer on Corporate Governance, Second Edition* by Cornelis A. de Kluyver
- *A Primer on Corporate Governance: Spain* by Felix Lopez-Iturriaga and Fern Tejerina-Gaite
- *A Primer On Corporate Governance: China* by Jean Jinghan Chen
- *Managerial Forensics* by J. Mark Munoz and Diana Heeb Bivona

# Announcing the Business Expert Press Digital Library

*Concise e-books business students need for classroom and research*

This book can also be purchased in an e-book collection by your library as

- a one-time purchase,
- that is owned forever,
- allows for simultaneous readers,
- has no restrictions on printing, and
- can be downloaded as PDFs from within the library community.

Our digital library collections are a great solution to beat the rising cost of textbooks. E-books can be loaded into their course management systems or onto student's e-book readers.
The **Business Expert Press** digital libraries are very affordable, with no obligation to buy in future years. For more information, please visit **www.businessexpertpress.com/librarians**. To set up a trial in the United States, please email **sales@businessexpertpress.com**.

www.ingramcontent.com/pod-product-compliance
Lightning Source LLC
Chambersburg PA
CBHW050105210326

41519CB00015BA/3839